ENTS

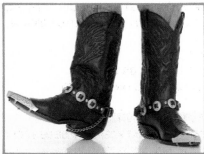
Printed and published by D.C. Thomson & Co., Ltd., 185 Fleet Street, London EC4A 2HS.
© D.C. Thomson & Co., Ltd., 1989.
ISBN 0-85116-444-7

£3.25

EXTRAS

SPITTING IMAGE

THIS might look like Marilyn Monroe but, believe it or not, this is actually a young lady by the name of Kay Kent. "It all started when I was at school", says Kay. "Somebody told me I looked a lot like Marilyn so I thought I'd make the most of it."

These days, Kay can make up to £1000 a day as a lookalike and now has an entire wardrobe full of Monroe-like clothing. However, the dress she's wearing here is the original thing and, as such, is worth a few bob! The look, from "Some Like It Hot", is probably Kay's most well known . . . she played the back of Marilyn's head in the Holsten Pils advert with Griff Rhys Jones!

JUNGLE MANIA

The leopard skin look is IN in a big way this year, so pop down to your local fabric store or jumble sale in search of some rather trendy scraps. Just sew on to your boring old accessories such as gloves or hats or form your own little masterpieces — such as a scarf or sash. Try draping a length of leopard fabric over the shoulder of a black top and simply secure with a brooch. Soon you will be looking grrr-oovy!

FACE UP TO IT!

Your face is probably your most important feature — it's the first thing people see, so you're not going to put any old thing on it, are you? We found five human guinea pigs to experiment with, spread funny smelling gunge on and then watch it crumble . . .

Tester: Pauline
Product: Body Shop "Camomile"
Verdict: This smelled of dried flowers which was OK at first but got really sickly after about ten minutes. Although it was especially for teenage skin, my face felt dry and broken when I took the pack off.

I doubt if I'd use it again; perhaps one of the other types the Body Shop do would suit my skin better, though.

Tester: Kerin
Product: Christie Lemon
Verdict: The first thing that I noticed about this pack was the citrus smell, and I'm afraid that's all that impressed me.

The sachet was boring and the face pack itself was gungey and difficult to put on as it smeared all over the place.

After all the hassle, I didn't even feel that it did my face any good so it was a waste of money really.

Tester: Susan
Product: Hot Pak
Verdict: This was really different from any face pack I'd tried before because I had to heat it under a hot tap before applying it.

It felt strange on my face because it was warm and I could practically feel my pores being cleaned.

It left my face feeling really tight and a little dry but once I'd moisturised my skin it felt a lot better.

Tester: Shona
Product: Christie Oatmeal
Verdict: This looks strange because it has little pieces of oatmeal in it, I felt they were rough on my face but, as long as I didn't rub too vigorously, it was OK. It took quite a while to dry and ended up cracking all over the place before I was finished.

It left me feeling refreshed and clear, but my shirt was covered with pieces which had flaked off!

Tester: Gillian
Product: Mudd Mask
Verdict: This was a really yukky colour but I didn't let that put me off. It went on quite smoothly and dried very quickly,, pulling my skin a bit (at least I knew it was doing something!).

I don't know if it helped my complexion or not, but my face did feel a lot smoother when I had finished.

Mark Jones, of Perfect Day, gets quite Santa-mental about Christmas of old. Witness...

"I can remember not being able to sleep at all on Xmas Eve and staying awake as long as I could. I even used to leave a glass of milk and some biscuits for Santa, totally unaware that my dad used to scoff them. I remember one Xmas Eve, I woke up to find my dad lurking at the bottom of my bed and I shouted at him 'cos I thought he was trying to steal my presents!"

Well?... don't say we didn't warn you!

PERFECT XMAS!

MAKE THIS THE YEAR YOU...

... Spice up your life with activities that are exciting, interesting, memorable or just plain mad! Like —

● Asking out that guy who makes your eyes boggle!
● Scribbling to worldwide penfriends (all the funkier if they reside somewhere really worth visiting like Fiji, Memphis, Paris, Florence . . .)
● Achieving your personal 'pretty potential' with a flattering hair-crop, exercise plan, clothes re-think, etc.
● Making the world a better place — get stuck into worthwhile causes such as Friends of the Earth, Greenpeace, World Wildlife Fund, Save the Children.
● Parading round town with a mate on Saturday afternoon in the naffest outfits you can dredge up — for a laugh!
● Trying to decide what you want to do with your life, finding out how to go about it and with hard work (eek!) making sure you achieve it.

The world's your oyster, girlies — go for it!!

Sleeping Beauty

OK, so you usually come in from the disco, hurl your clothes into the nearest corner and throw yourself, exhausted, under your duvet. But when going to bed *doesn't* entail a race against the clock, try these tips to keep you pretty as you slumber!

* Go through your usual cleansing, toning and moisturing routine then firm up face, by tapping round it with fingertips and up along cheek-bones.

* Coat your eyelashes in Vaseline to restore moisture and to prevent brittle lashes caused by wearing mascara.

* Your face isn't the only place where spots can erupt — backs are also in danger! Use a face mask as you would normally — except smoothed evenly on to your shoulders and upper back.

* Floss your teeth every time you brush them to remove embedded plaque.

* Gently brush your lips with a soft toothbrush to get rid of any dead skin, then stick on some Vaseline to soften them up.

* Rub in some body lotion in all those areas prone to dryness, such as elbows, knees and hands. Massage the fingers from the base to the tip to increase circulation and so encouraging nail growth.

* Push back cuticles with an orange stick or a cotton bud soaked in cuticle remover.

* And finally, if you have trouble sleeping, give yourself sweet dreams with a scent-sprayed pillow!

STRESS BUSTERS

If you find yourself rushing from classroom to classroom, dropping your books and tripping over your laces, then it sounds about time you learned to relax.

* Studying and exams are always a stressful time so set aside time at various points through the day to calm down.

* Take up yoga which will ease away all the tension from muscles and the mind — going to classes is the best way to learn.

* Meditation removes all thoughts from your mind and so helps you to wind down. Your local library will have books on meditation to teach you how.

* If you tend to bottle things up, talk to somebody close. You'll feel much better.

* Get fit! If you are a reasonable weight and take some form of regular exercise, you are less likely to feel under pressure.

* Often problems seem to mount up when you are tired, but rather than sitting around with your feet up, it's a better idea to go for a swim or even go out for the evening and enjoy yourself.

* If you feel you are overworked, organise yourself better. Draw up a chart to set specific times for homework or studying.

* While you're sitting at your desk, simple relaxing techniques can be practised. Try relaxing each muscle in turn and concentrate particularly on muscles around the face.

* And finally, when you feel things are getting on top of you, take a few seconds to breathe in and out deeply and try to put things into perspective.

   Chill out, daddio!

THE ALTERNATIVE VEGGIE

Whether you're a once-a-week veggie or are completely devoted to the vegetarian diet, it'll do you the world of good — if you eat sensibly. If you decide to turn vegetarian, there are usually problems when the rest of your family are stuck-in-their-way meat-eaters.

This often results in the vegetarian sitting at the dinner table with only half a plateful — eating the same as the rest of the family but without the meat. This is not only boring but dangerous as it's likely you won't be receiving enough vitamins and minerals. If you're determined to join the Morrisseys of the world, then talk it over with your family and come to some sort of arrangement. Perhaps you could write down a list of food you would like (look out for vegetarian cook-books in your library), or offer to make your own meals.

And remember, turning vegetarian doesn't mean either beans on toast or nut cutlets at every meal. With a bit of practice, you'll soon be dishing out one new and exciting meal after another!

STRANGE BUT TRUE!

Oh, my goodness! Who are these spotty youths? Surely this can't be one of the world's greatest stadium rock bands?

Actually, it is! This is none other than a young U2 somewhere in the back streets of Dublin. In those days, Ireland's Mr Rock was an aspiring Beatnik whose interest in roots ended where his hairdresser started.

Everyone's entitled to a dodgy shearing at one time or another, though!

TOP TEN
PRETTY HORRIBLE
CHRISTMAS PRESENTS
TO RECEIVE

1. Shakin' Stevens Album.
2. Bottle of El Pongo Eau de Cologne.
3. Box of 'Good Boy' Doggy chocs. (Oops, wrong stocking!)
4. Turquoise and orange Fair Isle sweater.
5. Initialled handkerchief.
6. Socks with individual toes.
7. Plastic jewellery.
8. Pathetic joke book.
9. Oven glove.
10. Jigsaw.

FOUR SEASONS BEAUTY

SPRING

Anything goes for the spring, as long as its au naturel. That doesn't mean to say it's time to face the world spots a-bared, it just calls for a bit of subtlety! First, a touch of concealer on those blemishes and dark rings under the eyes, then a layering of foundation and light dusting of powder to seal. Use a very light dusting of rosy blusher along the cheekbones (remember too little is better than too much). Enlarge eyes with a coating of mascara, either brown or transparent — black will look too harsh. Lip balm will finish this fresh-faced look.

As for clothes, get back to basics with a crisp white shirt, a denim jacket and top it off with a brightly coloured neck-scarf. Spring is also as good a season as any to get ahead with a hat. With looks like these, it'll certainly put a spring in your step!

SUMMER

Clothes-wise, anything bright and breezy goes for summer and sarongs or any form of body wrap are annual style-stealers — especially in sunny shades of yellow and orange. If you're at the beach, protect your hair from drying out and your skin from burning with a brimmed straw hat — they also look rather trendy!

Make-up is sultry with emphasis on only one feature for maximum effect. Create a perfect pout with brightly coloured lippy and play down the eyes, so as not to detract from those stunning smackers. If eyes are your best features, however, vice versa will apply. Keep skin as fresh and as clear of make-up as you can — using only a tinted moisturiser if necessary. And, remember, drinking lots of water will rid your skin of any impurities — about 6 glasses a day will work wonders.

AUTUMN

Autumn is time to get back to nature with browns, olive and russet-tones. Clothes should be flowing, such as long skirts and comfy, baggy sweaters. A pair of tan mountaineering-style boots will go well with most outfits.

Autumn beauty should be subtle but striking. A russet-toned lippy will also come in handy as a blusher this season and eyes look nice widened with a browny eyeliner and mascara.

Hair should be natural-looking. If you've got mid-length to long hair, use lots of mousse to scrunch dry. For extra waves, use a hot brush or even roll up sections of hair in ribbons and go to bed for ready-made curls in the morning. If you've got short hair, sleek it back with some gel for the natural-but-very-sophisticated look. Whatever the length of your hair, a scarf either holding it up in a ponytail or as a bandana will look great!

WINTER

You might think fashion disappears when the duffle coats come out in winter — but make this year an exception!

Look cosy in thick but colourful sweaters and co-ordinate with a bright scarf, gloves and hat. When you get up in the cold grey mornings, forget your usual long black coat and boots and opt for lots of red, purple, yellow and other cheerful colours to brighten up your day.

Use a good moisturiser to prevent your skin being damaged by the cold and a light layering of foundation and rosy blusher will guarantee that you don't merge in with the snow! Always wear a lip salve under your lip-stick before going outdoors to avoid dehydrating and chapping — and that would be no good for this mistletoe season, would it?!

7

ACTING

Even superstars have to wake up sometime — but it's not too awful getting up when you can lounge around in glam nightwear like this. Look out for slinky draped nighties, satin pyjamas and full-length wraps for your own star style!

UP!

When one's a famous actress, dahling, one spends the day like this . . .!

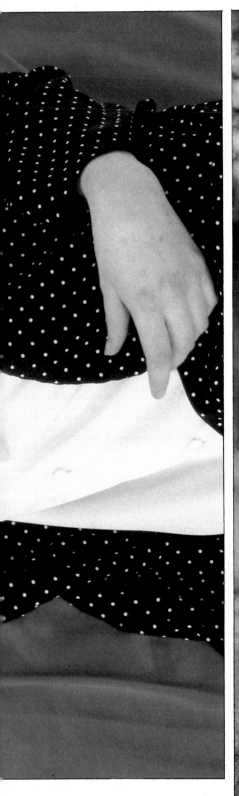

Even when out walking their pampered pooches, stars have to look good. You never know when an autograph hunter's going to pop out from behind a bush, do you? Go for smart trousers, classic blouses and maybe a stylish, plain woolly if there's a bit of a chill in the air!

9

A glamour girl's shopping is never done — and a classy suit in an unusual colour is just the thing for a girl about town to be seen in. The smartest suits have fitted jackets and on-the-knee skirts, with clean, simple lines to slim down any curvy bits!

When it comes to a night on the town, glamour is the all-important word. Go for shimmering silks and satins in strong jewel colours like ruby, emerald and sapphire, and don't forget the essential accessories — a smart handbag, low-heeled court shoes and tasteful jewellery.

Nightwear, Marks and Spencers; all other clothes from Top Shop.
Thanks to the Hotel de France, Edinburgh.

10

NOT VERY ATTRACTIVE CHAPS

(WHO'VE MADE IT BIG, NEVERTHELESS)!

SO YOU FANCY MATT GOSS BUT YOUR BOYFRIEND LOOKS MORE LIKE A CROSS BETWEEN A WEASEL AND A HALF-CHEWED JAM BUTTY?

DON'T WORRY — EVEN THE STARS AREN'T ALL BEAUTIES. TAKE A LOOK AT THESE FAMOUS UGS AND SEE WHAT WE MEAN!

Shane McGowan from the Pogues — possibly the ugliest man in the entire cosmos.

If snotty noses and fluorescent warts were 'in', Gilbert would be the most swoonsome guy this century. Unfortunately for him, they're not!

Charlie and Craig Proclaimer demonstrate what that fine Scottish air and a daily bowl of porridge can do for a man. So, be warned!

12

One buck-toothed Freddie Mercury was bad enough — but hundreds of them? Aaaghh, help!

Marc Almond, the original chinless wonder. Even all that make-up couldn't make him look any prettier!

Rowan Atkinson. Mmm — well, his earlobes are very nice! What more can we say?

Billy Bragg. In the Mr Ugly stakes, Comrade Billy wins by a nose. A very large nose, that is!

Here's our George. This man's got so many chins, he needs a bookmark to find his necklace.

For ape impressions, Tom's our fave. Dig that gleaming medallion, man! Groovy.

13

LONELY THIS

IT WAS A PRETENCE SARA HAD TO KEEP UP. SHE'D LOST BOBBY, BUT AT THE VERY LEAST, SHE COULD KEEP A LITTLE PRIDE . . .

HALF past five on Christmas Eve. The traffic was easing off, shops were closing and the streets were filled with people going home. Sara half closed her eyes on the scene below the flat window. Not much longer now, and Liz would be gone. Then she could stop pretending.

"Was that the post? I wondered if there'd be a delivery before I left."

Liz came out of the bedroom carrying her suitcase, her blue eyes wide and innocent. She looked gorgeous like that, the big fur hood framing her face, her golden hair escaping in soft tendrils. Sara felt unhappiness welling up inside her. No wonder she had lost Bobby to Liz — she was so beautiful.

"Are you expecting anything in particular?" Sara asked. "I could send it on to you at Bobby's if you'll be there all week."

"No! It doesn't matter that much." Liz smoothed the effect of her sudden exclamation with a smile. "It was just a thought."

Distantly, a clock struck the half hour. "You'll miss your bus," Sara pointed out.

"Yes, I'd better be going." Liz turned to pick up her heavy suitcase and glanced at Sara thoughtfully. "You're catching the six-thirty train home, aren't you? Have a lovely Christmas, and give my love to your family."

Again Sara felt a surge of sadness and wished Liz would just go away and leave her alone.

"I'll be thinking of you," Liz added. There was a slight strained pause, for they both understood the lie. Once she was with Bobby, she wouldn't think of anyone else.

Liz had been looking forward to this Christmas for weeks, every little detail planned. A whole new wardrobe. Presents galore for Bobby. It was going to be wonderful.

For Sara, the flat seemed to shrink once Liz had gone, the untidiness left by her packing only emphasising its emptiness. No one would have guessed it was Christmas. They had agreed there was no point in decorating the place as they were both going to be away. But there was no need to pretend any more, Sara thought.

She wasn't going home at all. She was staying here for the whole of the Christmas holidays, quite alone. She couldn't go home now even if she wanted to. Her parents were on a cruise. Way back in the summer, they had asked her if she wanted to join them, but she had refused. Those had been the days when Bobby had been hers. And Bobby had wanted her all to himself for Christmas.

"Christmas will be lovely," he had whispered. "We'll spend it together, you and I."

But that was before she'd brought him back to the flat and he'd seen Liz

for the first time, and she'd lost him.

Sara began to unpack her suitcase, part of the charade begun for Liz's benefit, then she sat down heavily on the bed. After all, there was no rush. She had all week to unpack. Nowhere to go, no one to see, all their college friends had gone home for the holidays. And, as she looked round with the prickling of tears behind her eyes, she couldn't imagine a more desolate, lonely place to spend Christmas.

But at least she didn't have to pretend any more and didn't have to listen to Liz's excited plans for her holiday, bursting with the joy of seeing Bobby again.

Right from the start, she had managed to conceal from Liz how much it had hurt losing Bobby. Bobby had never seemed to realise either. He had explained to Sara in his quiet, confident way that what had happened to him and Liz was inevitable. He and Liz had been instantly attracted to each other, and Sara could at least be sensible about it.

There had been a time when she suspected Bobby was a louse; that it hadn't been so much instant attraction as a game, that it didn't matter to Bobby if anyone got hurt. She had even thought that Liz would eventually lose him too, but time had proved her wrong. Even when Bobby's job had taken him North and he'd moved away, their love seemed as strong as ever. Things had been easier for Sara because he wasn't around any more, but Liz's happy visits to his new flat had proved regular reminders to Sara of how much she had lost.

And when Christmas approached, and Liz began making her ecstatic plans, Sara's looming lonely Christmas had taken on a pitiful aspect, and she had had to pretend that she had a wonderful family gathering to look forward to.

She heard the clank of the letterbox downstairs with a start of surprise. That must have been the late delivery Liz was talking about. She ran down the quiet staircase, aware of the empty rooms in the house, and her eyes

blurred again as she pulled at the thick brown envelope stuck in the letterbox. As she tugged with some force, the envelope ripped and the contents spilled out.

She paused, looking in puzzlement at the distinctive black scrawl on the envelope — Bobby's handwriting, addressed to Liz. And at her feet, six of the pale yellow envelopes Liz always used. Unopened letters from her to Bobby.

Consternation took the place of puzzlement. Why had he returned her letters? And as she bent down to pick them up, she couldn't help seeing the scrap of paper pinned to one of them.

LIZ, I'M SORRY. BUT YOU MUST BE SENSIBLE ABOUT THIS.

PLEASE DON'T WRITE AGAIN, AS IT UPSETS LOUISE.

BOBBY.

For a few seconds she was stunned, her mind racing through all the possibilities that the note raised. But there was only one certainty, and one that she couldn't quite understand. For Liz had gone — gone to spend Christmas with Bobby. Hadn't she?

Suddenly, there was the grating of the key in the lock. Sara turned to face the front door as it swung open, and watched disbelievingly as she saw Liz lifting her heavy suitcase in, her fur hood thrown back and her hair damp with snowflakes.

And then Liz stopped too, shocked to see Sara standing there.

"I . . . I thought you'd have gone to catch your train by now . . ." Liz began, then stopped, trapped.

"Did you come back for these?" Sara asked quietly, holding out the letters.

Liz stared for a long moment, then sank on to the bottom stair and put her head in her hands. "I never went to see him," she sighed. "It was all a . . . charade."

Sara sat beside her, in the shadows of the dimly lit hall, which couldn't quite disguise the tear stains on Liz's face.

"I couldn't tell you he'd found someone else," Liz went on in a hoarse voice. "Not after all I said about

14

CHRISTMAS

everlasting love . . . and what we did to you. Oh, I know you said he wasn't important, and Bobby said you'd be so sensible about it . . . but I knew you cared. And then when I got the first signals . . . you know . . . little things . . . hints that he didn't feel the same any more . . . I just couldn't tell you."

"I would have understood," Sara told her. "It happened to me first, remember?"

Liz looked at her guiltily, tears brimming in her eyes. "But you'd started to pick up the pieces again — you were so looking forward to Christmas. And I'd made so many plans for being with Bobby, I just kept on hoping and praying that even at the last moment, he might change his mind. In the end, it was easier just to keep on pretending."

Their eyes met.

"I was going to come back here and spend Christmas alone, after you'd gone," Liz said in puzzlement. "But you're still here. What happened? Did you miss your train?"

"I wasn't going anywhere either," Sara confessed with a distant smile. "And I didn't want to tell you."

There was a long, thoughtful silence.

"Got any food in?" Liz asked eventually.

Sara shook her head. "Not much. I couldn't really, not after telling you I was going home. You'd have noticed."

Liz grinned as she bent down to unlock her suitcase. "You're not as resourceful as me," she murmured, flipping back the lid. Sara, after a first glance of surprise, began to smile. A plump Christmas pudding lay inside, along with a frozen chicken and some mince pies.

"I wondered why it was so heavy," she said softly, and they both began to laugh, but uncertainly, because tears weren't far away. "Oh, Liz, we've not been very sensible about this after all, have we?"

"He was a bit of a louse," Liz said.

"Yeah, I'm beginning to think so, too."

"I think we ought to celebrate, in spite of him." Liz smiled. "We'll need lots of food!"

"Well," Sara mused, "if we're quick, we'll get to the supermarket before it closes."

"We'll get some nuts." Liz stood up, pulling her hood round her eyes. "Chocolates. Pickles."

"Fruit — and a cake!" Sara added, with rising excitement.

"And some decorations." They stood for a moment, smiling at each other, before Liz reached out and grabbed Sara's arm.

"Come on, we're wasting time!"

And they ran out of the door together, helter skelter in a flurry of snow, almost as if they were afraid that if they didn't hurry, Christmas would pass them by after all. □

TOUCHING SHORT STORY BY DENISE LEPPARD

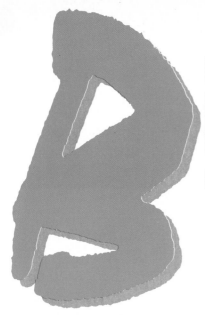

HAVE A
EAUTIFUL

● NO, WE DON'T GIVE UP EASILY, DO WE? STRUGGLING FORTH IN THE NEVER-ENDING TASK OF MAKING OUR READERS LOOK EVEN LOVELIER, WE'VE PUT TOGETHER THE JACKIE 1990 BEAUTY CALENDAR. FOLLOW THIS GUIDE TO LOOKING GOOD AND WE CAN GUARANTEE THAT YOU'LL TURN MORE THAN A FEW HEADS THIS YEAR!

FEBRUARY

Time to brighten up dull winter skin with a really deep cleanse. Why not steam your face? First, remove any make-up with a gentle cleanser, then, covering your head and shoulders with a towel, lean over a bowl of steaming hot water. Keep your face at least six inches away from the water to avoid burning your skin. After six or seven minutes, cleanse your face again, then moisturise.

MARCH

Spring cleaning time! Why not clean out your make-up kit and chuck out anything you don't use any more? To avoid clutter, just keep the essentials in your make-up bag — for example: concealer, foundation, loose powder, blusher, eyeshadow, mascara, lipstick and applicators. You'll notice that everything is so much easier if you're organised and don't have to scrabble around among tons of make-up to find what you're looking for.

JANUARY

After all the hassle of Christmas and New Year, why not have a relaxing weekend to recover, relax and psyche yourself up for the year ahead? A couple of early nights, a warm scented bath and hours and hours in front of the fire will make you feel soothed, contented and ready for anything. Why not take this opportunity to cleanse your system by eating only fresh fruit, vegetables and high-fibre foods? Drink plenty of water, too.

YEAR

APRIL

We're well into the school year now and you're probably working really hard. Don't overdo it, though — try to have at least one early night a week. If you have difficulty sleeping, some gentle exercise earlier on in the evening, then an hour or two reading or listening to records should relax you. If you still find it difficult to get up, a good early morning wakener is to drink a glass of hot water with a slice of lemon — it'll cleanse the system, too!

MAY

If you want your tan to last longer this year, make sure your skin is in peak condition before you go anywhere near the sun. Give yourself a weekly body scrub in the bath or use a friction glove or loofah to slough off dead skin and get your circulation going. As always, moisturise with a body lotion after showering or bathing to replace lost moisture.

JUNE

Time to bare those legs, so make sure they look smooth and fuzz-free. The most effective method of hair removal is waxing and it's easily done at home with a home waxing kit. Your legs must be clean and dry, otherwise the wax won't stick to them. Press on the strip, then rip it off sharply in an upwards direction. Your legs will feel quite tender for a while afterwards, but you can cool them by smothering them with some moisturiser. You'll be glad to hear that you won't have to repeat this until six weeks later, as regrowth is quite slow.

JULY

Moisturise sun-dried skin with a home-made face mask. Cleanse your skin first with a mild soap or cream cleanser, then pat gently dry with a soft towel. Next, mash a banana with a tablespoonful of honey and a beaten egg, apply to your face and leave for fifteen minutes.

AUGUST

Your hands and nails can suffer in hot weather, so it's a good idea to give yourself a simple manicure every now and then. Just soak your fingertips in warm, soapy water, remove any dirt from under the nails, then use an orange stick to push back your cuticles.

SEPTEMBER

After the summer, your hair may be dried or damaged due to the sun. Why not try an oil treatment to give it some life and sheen? Warm some olive oil (you can do this by putting the oil in a cup which is sitting in a bowl of hot water) and massage this in to your hair and scalp. Wrap your head in a hot, damp towel, and leave for at least half an hour. Shampoo twice and rinse very well, then condition with your usual conditioner.

OCTOBER

At this time of year, your feet are being stuffed in to clumpy shoes and boots, so it's important to take extra care of them. If you find the skin on your feet is becoming dry and rough, give them a scrub with a pumice stone in the bath, dry them thoroughly then smother them with lots of moisturiser.

NOVEMBER

November's quite a dull, drizzly month — so what better way to brighten it up than dyeing your hair? No, it doesn't have to be permanent — that should be left to the professionals — but there are some very good temporary colours on the market. First wash your hair with a gentle shampoo, then after towel drying your hair, apply the colour all over, brushing through with a round brush to ensure an even coverage. Leave on for the suggested time, then rinse your hair thoroughly and apply conditioner. Leave this on for a few minutes, as hair colourants can be quite drying. Style your hair with the minimum use of heated appliances, ie. hairdryer, hotbrush. Avoid colourants if your hair is bleached or permed — the result could be disastrous.

DECEMBER

Now that we're well into winter, it's essential (unless you want to look like a shedding lizard!) that your skin is kept soft and protected. Use a cream cleanser applied with a complexion brush to stimulate circulation, and a good moisturiser during the day and at night. To avoid cracked lips and cold sores, keep your lips protected with Vaseline, a good lip balm or a moisturising lipstick. If the skin on your lips is already flaking off, apply Vaseline then rub gently with a soft toothbrush. This'll make your lips smooth and kissable, so you can be sure your pout is perfect when the mistletoe comes round!

DOING THE BUSINESS

When it comes to jobs and careers, some people know exactly what they want and they'll work their very hardest to get where they want to go. We visited four up-and-coming stars in their profession and asked them about their work, how they started and how they mean to go on . . .

NAME: SAMANTHA CAIRNEY
AGE: SEVENTEEN
OCCUPATION: MODEL

"I was more or less tricked into becoming a model. My dad sent away photographs of me to a model agency and they accepted me — without my knowledge at all. It was a bit of a shock, but I soon got used to it.

"My mum and dad were really enthusiastic about me modelling and my friends were pretty amazed that I had been accepted.

"To begin with I got basic catwalk training, posture control and all that, but, really, training is continuous and mistakes will always be made. I was really frightened at first because I had no confidence and was scared stiff in case I made a mess of things. Luckily, I haven't had any really bad experiences yet. Anyway, once you get used to it, you relax and this is reflected in the photo which looks more natural and professional.

"I really enjoy my work, it's good fun even if it's not as glamorous as everyone expects it to be. It's difficult to keep looking your best at times, especially when you're freezing to death in the wind and rain. The hours are hard — it can be a ten-hour day sometimes. Having said that, I really enjoy my work. I know it's really clichéd but I enjoy meeting new people and it makes all the difference when you have to work with people who are nice. It also makes it easier to smile through all those photos!

"Although I'm going to work in Japan for a few months, which I'm really looking forward to, I don't really see modelling as a long-term career — I'll carry on as long as I'm happy with it and I'm getting work."

NAME: ASTRA DEVEREUX
AGE: SIXTEEN
OCCUPATION: HAIRDRESSER

"I was always really interested in hairdressing — even at school I was trimming all of my friends' hair — so becoming a hairdresser seemed the natural thing to do. To begin with, I got a lot of encouragement from my friends and family but when I got a job here in Vidal Sassoon, they were really pleased for me. It's a great chance for me to get the best training around and that's what I've always wanted — I don't want to be average.

"Although I had done some hairdressing before I joined the company, the training programme presumes you know nothing, so you start from scratch. That means learning all of the cutting and styling techniques again and picking up new and better ways. It seems really different to start with and it's quite confusing but, now I'm into the swing of things, I already feel that I'm a much better hairdresser than I was when I came here.

"The first time I cut hair here I was really nervous, despite knowing that I'd done it well in the past. I knew I was capable of doing it but it's pretty nerve-wracking with the chief stylist watching over!

"All in all, I feel privileged to be working for such a respected company — it's really exciting to know that I'm getting the best training and that means I'm getting the best start in the business.

"It's my ambition to branch out on my own once I have a few years' training and experience behind me, perhaps to open my own salon eventually. I'll keep my fingers crossed!"

NAME: HELEN WATSON
AGE: NINETEEN
OCCUPATION: VETERINARY NURSE

"I never really planned a career in veterinary nursing — I ended up here by accident. I'd originally intended being a secretary but, as luck would have it, I ended up in this practice as their assistant. I've always loved animals so I suppose it was fate that I landed here.

"My parents really left me to do what I wanted, but they were really thrilled when I got this job and that made it even more worthwhile.

"Working here is all part of my training — I serve some time here for practical experience and then go on to college for about three years of theory and loads of exams.

"The surgery is fascinating; as well as helping out at reception, I work in the pharmacy — learning about diseases and their treatments. The most satisfying part of the job has to be nursing the animals, though. We have a hospital here and everyone shares the responsibility of cleaning, feeding and nursing the animals. It's not all cuddling cute kittens, that's for sure!

"It's great when the animals start to get better but I get really upset if they don't do well and I usually go home at night and take my frustration out on my brothers! Obviously, I'll get a bit tougher as I get used to the work but I don't think I'll ever be able to just shrug things off!

"Sometimes I think I'm too emotional for this job and I often end up taking a particularly deserving patient home. So far I've got a gerbil, Robert, a dog, Hilda, and a cat called James. My latest 'baby' is McGregor, a little kitten someone brought in. He'd either been in an accident or else he'd been badly treated by his owners. He was in a real state when he came to us but he's come on great now and I'm working on my mum and dad to see if I can keep him!"

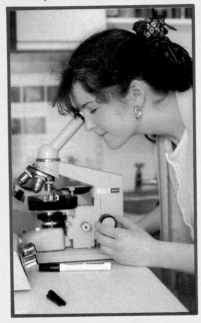

NAME: FRANCES McGECHIE
AGE: TWENTY-TWO
OCCUPATION: POLICEWOMAN

"I know it sounds corny, but I always wanted to be a policewoman, even when I was still at primary school, so it was a real achievement when I was accepted into the police force.

"Now, I'm almost at the end of my two year 'probationary' or training period. It's been really hard work because, right from day one, I was involved in 'real' police work. During the two years, there are three local courses and four at Tulliallan, the Scottish police training centre, and all of them have exams at the end. I'm coming up to my final confirmation exam and that's going to be really difficult because I'll be tested on everything I've learned in training.

"The probationary period has got to be difficult because we have to be fully prepared in all sorts of situations.

"Sometimes things can get a bit hairy — I'm on the Fast Action Response Team, that means that we get called out to a lot of fights and potentially dangerous situations. Being a woman can have its advantages though, because we often diffuse fights as not many men, no matter how drunk or macho they may be, will hit a woman.

"Obviously it's scary going into danger but I need to feel a little frightened — if I don't, my adrenalin doesn't get going and that could make me slower to react and more vulnerable. I have to keep my wits about me for the sake of my colleagues as well as myself. We're like the three musketeers at times, so we all tend to look after one another.

"I suppose you'll be able to tell how much I love my job by now! I get a lot of pleasure and satisfaction from doing the job well and I think my main ambition is to get through my probation and be accepted as a good police officer."

Compatible Couple

Dangerous Duo

Doubtful but Possible

	ARIES	TAURUS	GEMINI	CANCER	LEO	VIRGO
ARIES	Unfortunately you are both very dominant and forceful.					
TAURUS	Excellent match, but watch your temper!	Both can be jealous and stubborn — but both will forgive easily, too.				
GEMINI	Emotional Aries may be too intense for practical Gemini.	Not a very good match. Taurus is too practical for Gemini.	You're very compatible — you have the same emotional needs.			
CANCER	Difficult companions. You both have very different attitudes.	You'll be very happy together, if Taurus is careful not to hurt sensitive Cancer's feelings.	The Cancerian should watch out for Gemini's moody spells.	A lovely match — you both want the same things from each other.		
LEO	Great couple — so long as Leo is the centre of attention!	You'll both understand the sensitive side of your partner. A good couple.	Brash Leo is far too loud for the more reserved Gemini.	Leo should try to be patient with Cancer's moods. Otherwise, a good combination.	This pair of star signs are often very happy together, but you'll probably both be fighting for the limelight all the time!	
VIRGO	Fine, so long as Virgo doesn't nag too much!	Possible — so long as Taurus can ignore Virgo's criticism.	This relationship will start well, but fizzle out quite soon as boredom settles in.	The Cancerian's probably a bit too shy for Virgo, who prefers a more direct approach.	This will probably be a fairly dull relationship as you don't have much in common.	This would be a continual battle of wits — and nerves. Not usually a successful combination!
LIBRA	Wonderful couple. Warm, passionate Libra will calm the fiery Aries.	A perfect match, you'll never get bored with each other's company.	An ideal couple. You share the same interests and will love being together.	Be prepared for long days of silence as both of you have a natural ability for sulking!	Both of you love flattery and a rich lifestyle. So long as you've plenty of money, you'll have a great time!	Libra will find it very difficult to take Virgo's constant criticism.
SCORPIO	Unfortunately, both of you will want to dominate.	You've got a lot in common but both must overcome jealousy and learn to trust each other.	This relationship will have its ups and downs, but will always end happily.	Ideal couple. Each has a lot of love to give and you'll be quite happy with only each other for company.	A good relationship if Leo is allowed to be the boss.	A good match. Each has a very quick wit, so there'll be lots of laughs.
SAGITTARIUS	Ideal couple. Both of you want the same things out of life.	The flirty Sagittarian may be too much for the possessive Taurean to cope with.	You go well together. You're both outspoken and love wild nights out!	Sagittarius can be flirty — it may be a good idea for Cancer not to get too involved until they feel the Sagittarian's trustworthy.	Both of you love life and will have an exciting and full-of-surprises relationship.	Good match, if Virgo can stop nagging.
CAPRICORN	Aries may be too impatient for easy-going Capricorn.	Both signs love flattery and encouragement and love will last if you don't take each other for granted.	This relationship might work — but only if Capricorn tries not to be too domineering.	A happy, steady relationship with complete trust on both sides.	Leo will forgive and forget, but any disagreements will be long-remembered by Capricorn.	Usually a good match. You both take pride in yourselves and your surroundings.
AQUARIUS	Dreamy Aquarius will irritate ambitious Aries.	Taurus might be too laid back for the Aquarian.	A lively relationship with lots of laughs.	The Cancerian may be too home-loving for the vivacious Aquarian.	A good match. You understand each other totally.	This combination can be either very good or very bad. It does help if you go to the same school or have mutual friends.
PISCES	Pisces tends to be a bit too sentimental and sloppy for Aries.	You go together very well. You both want love and romance and should have a lasting relationship.	The Piscean will have to make an effort not to be too possessive for this to work.	This couple is likely to fall out often but will make up very quickly afterwards.	Pisces may be too sensitive for the loud-mouthed Leo.	These signs are complete opposites, but it all helps to make your relationship more interesting.

IT'S ALL IN THE STARS!

Will you be holding hands for ever or will you be baring teeth from the moment you meet?

OK, so your eyes have met across the classroom, you see passion in his eyes and you realise it's love at first sight. He's your perfect man — six foot tall, blue eyes, blond hair, enchanting smile and the most adorable way of squinting at the blackboard.

You imagine the two of you far away from this draughty classroom — on a sun-drenched beach, perhaps, or snuggled up in front of a roaring log fire.

But, wait a minute, before you get too carried away. How do you know you two are compatible? Maybe his idea of the perfect day out is letting you cheer him on at his footie game on Saturday, or even a fun-filled night at the local lapidary club. Not exactly a bundle of laughs!

So, to get the grotty details of his personality, just ask him what his star sign is. Back at your desk, whip out your groovy star-searching Jackie Annual, check our star-sign table and you'll soon know exactly whether or not he's worth lending your Biro to!

If you find you're a match made in heaven, the matching astrological waves will simply zap across the desks and an everlasting romance will have begun (fingers crossed)! BUT, if the worst comes to the worst, and your stars say you go together like a jam and gherkin sandwich, don't despair — the Capricorn of your dreams could be just around the corner!

To use the chart, simply run your finger along the bottom of the chart until you come to either his or your star sign and then up the side of the chart to find the other. Where the two meet, you'll find your destiny.

LIBRA	SCORPIO	SAGITTARIUS	CAPRICORN	AQUARIUS	PISCES
A good couple. You're very similar to each other and will enjoy the same entertainment.					
A nice couple, but beware of Scorpio trying to dominate.	Don't insult each other — Scorpio doesn't easily forgive.				
A perfect couple. You'll never run out of conversation.	Not too advisable. There could be mutual distrust and Scorpio's possessiveness will be unbearable.	OK short term, but Sagittarius isn't really keen on long relationships.			
You seem to be entirely opposite in your outlook, but you'll realise you have more in common as time goes by.	Not really emotionally compatible. Both of you will want the last word in arguments.	Capricorn is too pessimistic for the outgoing Sagittarius.	Both of you like planning for the future, so you can enjoy doing this together. A good couple.		
You're both very lovable people and like the same things in life.	Aquarius is a bit too stuffy for Scorpio's passionate nature.	Similar temperaments. Both of you love travel and the more exciting things in life.	Capricorn shouldn't try to tie down Aquarius who will want to get out and about.	Absolutely perfect for each other — you understand your partner and treat them accordingly.	
Sometimes, this couple find it hard to keep the relationship going. The Piscean's sulks will eventually get on Libra's nerves.	Love at first sight, perhaps, but it won't usually last.	Sagittarius will resent the Piscean trying to tie him down.	Capricorn will boost Pisces' confidence — and Pisceans love to feel needed.	A good couple. You're always willing to help and understand each other's difficulties.	You both have the same faults but also the same good qualities. You'll get on very well together.

continued overleaf

IT'S ALL IN THE STARS!

(continued from previous page)

Well, the proof of the pudding is in the eating(!), as they say. So is it true that your relationship is doomed from the start just because you're a nagging Virgo and he's a lazy Libra?

We took to the streets to ask you lot what you thought of all this star-gazing . . . !

Tony and Sharon

SHARON: "I've no idea what his star sign is."
TONY: "I've no idea what Sharon's sign is and I don't believe any of that rubbish, anyway!"

Jillian (Taurus) and Scott (Aquarius)

JILLIAN: "We're not supposed to make a good match but we don't believe in any of that, anyway. We get on absolutely brilliantly — so tell that to your horoscope writer!"

Murray (Taurus) and Annette (Taurus)

MURRAY: "We've been together for two whole years. Too long!"
ANNETTE: "What d'you mean 'too long'?! I'll see you about this later!

"Anyway, according to your chart, we're not supposed to be a good couple — but we prove it wrong. I do believe in most of the horoscope stuff, but not this one!"

Margaret (Aquarius) and David (Libra)

DAVID: "We've been going out for almost two years. Margaret's an Aquarius and I'm a Libran. Your chart says we should get on well and we do, but even if it said we were a terrible match, I wouldn't pay any attention. We think we're compatible and that's all that counts."

Dave (Aries) and Fiona (Cancer)

FIONA: "We've been going out for eight months. Dave's an Aries and I'm a Cancerian. I don't know if we're supposed to be compatible but we are, so there! We do believe in horoscopes and stuff, though."
DAVE: "Here, this chart says we're not compatible! What a load of rubbish!"

HOLLYWOOD

BRIGITTE · BARDOT

CLASSICS

DOUBLE TAKE

Just like in all the best television soaps, we offered Jacqueline and Mike, our not-very-brave volunteers, a cup of strong, sweet tea before they faced the ordeal of 'The Big Makeover'.
After Jacqueline had tired herself out after repeatedly screaming, "They won't cut my hair short, will they? Please tell me they won't cut my hair . . ." and Mike muttering, "They'd better not try to make me wear make-up . . ." etc. etc., we whisked them off to Vidal Sassoon in Glasgow.

Jacqueline putting on a brave face before the ord[e]

AFTER quite a bit of "No, you go first", Jacqueline was first in the hot seat.
The stylist, Tim Harley, took a lot of time talking to Jacqueline about her hair. Wanting to improve the texture of her hair while keeping the length, Jacqueline decided (after much "Oh, I don't really know!" and other similar Mavis Riley impressions) to have a perm.
Before she could change her mind, Tim trimmed her hair to get rid of the split ends — long hair needs trimming every six

There's no escape now as Tim gets started

weeks to prevent the hair from splitting, but with Jacqueline's fear of hairdressers (a common trait in those with long hair) she hadn't had her hair cut for months.
With scissors at the ready, Tim graduated the fringe down the sides for versatile styling, and tidied up the layers at the back.
Grace then took over to perform the

Mike also trying to look brave

And in with the curlers . . .

dried her hair using a diffuser (this ensures that there's no frizz), lifting the hair at the roots.

To finish with, Tim tipped Jacqueline's hair from side to side, spraying with hairspray to create a fuller look.

With the hair finished, it was now time to go on to the make-up.

Jacqueline's skin was in excellent condition, so she only needed a little concealer to cover the bags under her eyes (caused by too many late nights, no doubt!) and a light covering of foundation to even out her skin tone. A pale, pinky tone of loose powder sealed the colour.

A touch of rose-coloured blusher was brushed quite high on Jacqueline's cheeks to bring emphasis to her eyes and add a little shape to her face. Then some sugary pink eyeshadow was brushed onto Jacqueline's lids with a deeper pink blended into the sockets.

A dark brown eyeshadow was lightly brushed onto her eyebrows to fill them

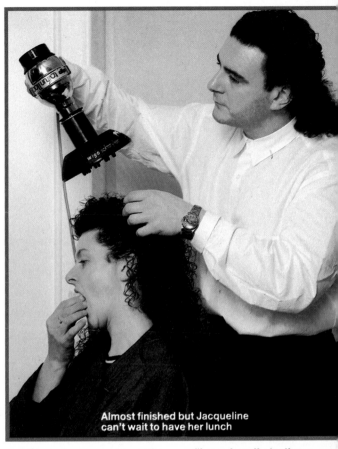

Almost finished but Jacqueline can't wait to have her lunch

out and a couple of coats of mascara onto her already dark lashes.

The look was finished with a shade of grape lipstick, brushed onto her lips.

So, the all-important question, what did Jacqueline think of the new her?

"I can hardly believe it! Is that really me? Yes, it certainly is an improvement. I can hardly get over my hair — it doesn't look lank any more, that's for sure!" (Hours more of disbelieving twitterings . . .)

Ah, well, yet another success story!

lengthy task of putting the curlers in and then taking them all out again a couple of hours later after the perming lotions had been applied and the hair had been rinsed.

By this time Jacqueline's stomach was rumbling, and, as you can see, she couldn't even stop stuffing her face to get her photo taken!

Next, Tim blow-

Mike — looking like he's about to get some teeth out ie. non-too-macho!

Meanwhile, as Jacqueline was receiving the final touches, it was on to Mike.

Mike's hair was quite short to begin with so Tim didn't really have much scope (or so we thought!).

After a good wash and conditioning — something Mike had never done to his hair before — Tim set to

continued overleaf

DOUBLE TAKE

continued from previous page

work turning Mike into a rather hunksome chap indeed!

To start with, Tim took a good inch or so off the top, getting rid of the floppy bits. The sides and the back were cropped short and clippers were used to ensure the cut was as even as possible.

The hair then graduated into a longer length at the top.

Tim left a longish bit at the front which he flicked to the right, adding a bit of frontal interest. Working through some gel, Tim smoothed Mike's hair to one side and back, giving a classy effect.

Not keen to be plastered in make-up, (as if we would!) a little concealer was applied under his eyes then a light colouring of foundation evened out Mike's skin tone. We added just a puff of powder to take away

Jacqueline's new glam look

In for the chop!

the shine.

Some clear mascara was stroked onto his lashes, making his eyes look a little bigger.

"I hate this make-up. I'm glad I'm not a girl," was his only comment about his face.

What about his hair?

"Oh, it'll take time to get used to it, but it's a nice cut."

Oh, this boy is oozing enthusiasm — there's just no pleasing some people, is there?!

Our thanks go to all the staff at Vidal Sassoon

A very relieved Mike looking rather suave

27

Here we go, pop- fans! Howzabout having a crack at our super pop quiz! It's sure to get your wee wheelies turning! Sorry, no prizes, but lots of peer group prestige!

A QUE

12. Which señora did Freddie Mercury record a series of duets with?
13. Bros, as Gloss, released a single called "Mystery Lady". True or false?

14. Of which group was Clark Datchler the vocalist?
15. Who shot to fame after dropping his trews in a Levi's commercial?
16. What is the name of Five Star's manager/dad?

1. Who are Neil Tennant and Chris Lowe better known as?
2. Where was Michael Jackson born?
3. Which American songstress made her film debut in "The Allnighter"?
4. Name three of the five legendary music men who formed The Travelling Wilburys.
5. Who produced "The Memphis Sessions" for Wet Wet Wet?
6. What was Madonna's maiden name?
7. Which member of Madness joined Voice Of The Beehive?
8. What do Max Headroom and Tom Jones have in common?
9. What was the name of Rick Astley's band before he hit the big time?
10. Who gave Sheena Easton her first big break?
11. When did George Michael and Andrew Ridgeley split up?

17. Name the band Pal and Mags had before meeting up with Morten and forming A-ha?
18. Who fronts The Plastic Population?
19. Which Aussie soap opera did Kylie Minogue star in?
20. Marti Pellow was born in a toilet. True or false?
21. Which band was Prince formerly a member of?

22. Which American comedy star appeared in Paul Simon's video for "You Can Call Me Al"?

23. Patsy Kensit appeared with which famous pop star in "Absolute Beginners"?

24. What was the name of the band that included both Belinda Carlisle and Jane Wiedlin?

25. Which pop star's real name is Stuart Goddard?

26. Which band replaced Eg with Steve?

27. What do the initials SAW stand for?

28. Which all-girl group encouraged lots of MP's to get down and boogie?

29. Who twisted away the pounds with Chubby Checker in the summer of '88?

30. Which overweight superstar made his final screen appearance in "Hairspray"?

31. What is Bono's real name?

32. Who was "The Hardline According To"?

33. What do George Michael and Annie Lennox have in common?

34. Which member of Bros isn't a twin?

35. What are the names of Michael Jackson's two sisters?

36. Who sang the theme tune to the cult TV show, "Moonlighting"?

37. Who promised "The First Of A Million Kisses"?

38. What's the surname of Ben from Curiosity Killed The Cat?

39. Which form of footwear did King and Alexei Sayle have in common?

40. Which larger-than-life American singer played Eddie in "The Rocky Horror Picture Show"?

41. With whom did Paul Weller sing before forming The Style Council?

42. Who helped Gary Glitter back to the top of the charts with a reworked version of "Rock and Roll Part II"?

43. Who, according to her Equity card, is known as Miss Sammy?

44. Name Dire Straits' best-selling, multi-platinum album.

45. Who duetted with David Bowie on "Little Drummer Boy"?

46. Who wrote the Band Aid single, "Do They Know It's Christmas?"?

47. Who "found" Elisa Fiorillo?

48. Which seaside resort does Chris Lowe come from?

49. What was the name of Phil Collins' first feature film?

50. Tracey and Melissa from Voice Of The Beehive are sisters. True or false?

ANSWERS

1. Pet Shop Boys.
2. Gary, Indiana.
3. Susannah Hoffs.
4. Bob Dylan, Tom Petty, Roy Orbison, George Harrison, Jeff Lynne.
5. Willie Mitchell.
6. Ciccone.
7. Woody (Daniel Woodgate), the drummer.
8. They both had hits with The Art Of Noise.
9. FBI.
10. Esther Rantzen on "The Big Time".
11. 1986.
12. Montserrat Caballe.
13. True.
14. Johnny Hates Jazz.
15. Nick Kamen.
16. Buster Pearson.
17. Bridges.
18. Yazz.
19. Neighbours.
20. True.
21. The Time.
22. Chevy Chase.
23. David Bowie.
24. The Go-Go's.
25. Adam Ant.
26. Brother Beyond.
27. Stock, Aitken and Waterman.
28. Bananarama.
29. The Fat Boys.
30. Divine.
31. Paul Hewson.
32. Terence Trent D'Arby.
33. They have both duetted with Aretha Franklin.
34. Craig Logan.
35. Janet and LaToya.
36. Al Jarreau.
37. Fairground Attraction.
38. Volpeliere-Pierrot.
39. Dr Marten boots.
40. Meatloaf.
41. The Jam.
42. The Timelords.
43. Samantha Fox.
44. Brothers In Arms.
45. Bing Crosby.
46. Midge Ure.
47. John 'Jellybean' Benitez.
48. Blackpool.
49. Buster.
50. True.

HOW YOU RATE

0-15

Well! Not, perhaps, the best score in the world but at least you were honest! Give up all ambitions of being the Pop Brain of Britain — try something like needlework!

16-36

A fair enough score — not too good, but not too bad, either! You might never be the most knowledgeable pop person on this earth but at least you're not a complete dunce.

36-50

Well done! You're either extremely brainy or a birrova cheat! We bet you've got a fairly brilliant record collection with not a Tiffany record in sight.

DESIGNER CHEAP

One of the reasons designer clothes are so expensive is because there are only a few made of that style. But you can still look really classy if you follow these guidelines.
* Choose simple, classic clothes in natural fabrics like wool, linen and cotton. Steer clear of the 'latest' fashions — they won't last long in the style stakes.
* Most colours are OK as long as the clothes are well dyed and the colour won't wash out. You can tell this by looking closely at the fabric. If there seems to be a layer

LET'S PRETEND

FOR THOSE OF US WHO CAN'T AFFORD THE REAL THING, GETTING HOLD OF A FAKE IS NO PROBLEM. NEARLY EVERYTHING HAS BEEN COPIED AT SOME TIME — CORNFLAKES, PAINTINGS, EVEN TOYS — SO IT'S NOTHING UNUSUAL WHEN SOMETHING 'RARE' SUDDENLY FLOODS THE MARKET. THERE'S NO SHAME IN WEARING FAKE BUT YOU DON'T WANT EVERYONE TO KNOW THAT'S WHAT IT IS! THE SECRET IS TO WEAR IT WITH STYLE . . .

of small white fibres lying on the surface, the colour won't last very long.

* Choose quality garments — they don't need to cost the earth. They should be well made and the material should be firmly woven. Avoid garments with puckered or badly finished seams, flaws in the fabric or dodgy fastenings.
* Make sure they fit perfectly. Nothing looks worse than really tight or baggy clothes.
* Accessories should be in neutral shades like cream or black or a strong colour, like red. Avoid garish tones as these look cheap and tacky.
* Underwear shouldn't show through. If you're wearing seamed stockings, make sure they're straight.
* Shoes shouldn't be too high — no-one looks stylish staggering about!

OUT OF A BOTTLE

Nearly all of the world's most famous blondes became so with the help of a bottle or two of peroxide! There's Marilyn Monroe, Jayne Mansfield, Samantha Fox and Paula Yates, and that's just for starters!

However, as with all things, if you're going to do it, do it right!

Firstly, you should avoid going blonde if you've permed, red, or very dark hair (that is, unless you don't mind getting your roots done every couple of months, or waking up one morning to find your hair lying on your pillow!).

Remember that when dyed hair grows, you're faced with a difficult decision — to get the roots done, cut the dyed bits off or look horrible for months while it grows.

If you've decided to go blonde, don't even consider doing it yourself — let the professionals do it!

Bleached hair looks best when it's short — it'll be easier to look after that way, too. Remember dyed hair needs lots of conditioning to stay looking shiny and soft.

WHAT A GEM

Costume jewellery is so like the real thing, that only close inspection reveals that it's nothing of the sort.

There are lots of speciality shops which sell costume jewellery, but these can be quite expensive. Look in second-hand shops and craft fairs for bargains.

When you're wearing it, don't go over the top — subtlety is best. Choose one interesting piece, rather than piling on tons of jewels!

WIG IT!

Wigs are fabulous if you've had a disaster at the hairdresser, if you couldn't be bothered doing your hair or if you just fancy a complete change.

There are loads of styles and colours to choose from, from wacky purple ones to hairpieces which match your hair colour exactly.

They're available from good accessory shops, theatrical suppliers and department stores, and shouldn't set you back too much.

FAKES AT YOUR FINGERTIPS

False fingernails have been around for decades, but it's only within the last few years that they've been developed to look more natural and — in some cases — to last.

Follow the instructions for application carefully and don't go over the top length-wise — the longer they are, the greater the chance of them flicking off.

If they're the un-coloured kind, paint them carefully, using a bright or strong coloured nail varnish, as paler shades make their falseness more obvious.

TWO-FACED

It isn't so much the brand of make-up you use as the way you apply it. It's true that sometimes, the more expensive kinds of make up contain better quality ingredients and can last longer, but usually, you're paying extra for the fancy packaging.

Create a classic make-up look using a pale foundation, making sure you conceal any blemishes or dark circles.

Use the minimum of blusher, concentrating on the cheekbones to draw attention to your eyes.

Highlight your brow bones and carefully blend a dark eyeshadow from your lashes, where it should be at its darkest, to the socket where it should disappear to nothing.

Using a little eyeshadow of the same colour, lightly brush some into your sockets. Don't underline your eyes, but use lashings of mascara. Accentuate your eyebrows, first by brushing with a brow brush, then lightly brushing on a dark shade of eyeshadow. Finish off with a deep tone of lipstick — red's ideal, but dramatic shades of purple, pink or rust look good, too. ●

HOLLYWOOD

JAMES·DEAN

CLASSICS

STAMP IT OUT!

"THATCHER AND GORBACHEV TO MEET TO DISCUSS EAST-WEST RELATIONS." HMM. I DON'T SUPPOSE THAT MEANS THEY'RE GOING TO TALK ABOUT GRAHAM AND ME! IT WOULD BE A LAUGH IF IT DID THOUGH, WOULDN'T IT?

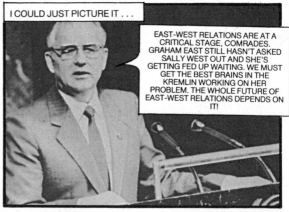

I COULD JUST PICTURE IT . . .

EAST-WEST RELATIONS ARE AT A CRITICAL STAGE, COMRADES. GRAHAM EAST STILL HASN'T ASKED SALLY WEST OUT AND SHE'S GETTING FED UP WAITING. WE MUST GET THE BEST BRAINS IN THE KREMLIN WORKING ON HER PROBLEM. THE WHOLE FUTURE OF EAST-WEST RELATIONS DEPENDS ON IT!

AFTER WORK . . .

MAYBE IT'S NOT SUCH A DAFT IDEA. I SAW A VIDEO A WHILE AGO ABOUT THIS LIVERPOOL GIRL WHO WAS HAVING A ROMANCE WITH A RUSSIAN SAILOR AND WROTE TO THE RUSSIAN PRESIDENT ABOUT IT. I COULD DO THE SAME, COULDN'T I?

SO . . .

I MEAN, IF WORLD LEADERS ARE SO GREAT AT SOLVING ALL THOSE BIG PROBLEMS, A LITTLE ONE LIKE MINE SHOULDN'T BE ANY TROUBLE FOR THEM!

AND . . .

I'M SENDING TWO LETTERS. ONE TO MRS THATCHER AND ONE TO MR GORBACHEV. I'VE JUST ASKED IF THEY'VE ANY IDEAS ABOUT HOW I CAN GET GRAHAM TO ASK ME OUT. I DON'T SUPPOSE THEY'LL BOTHER REPLYING, BUT IT'S WORTH A TRY.

I COULD JUST IMAGINE WHAT WOULD HAPPEN . . .

COMRADE SALLY. THERE IS ONLY ONE WAY TO WIN THIS BOY'S HEART. YOU MUST TRY A LITTLE PERESTROIKA ON HIM. OPENNESS IS WHAT COUNTS IN ANY RELATIONSHIP . . .

DEAR SALLY. I'M SORRY TO HEAR ABOUT YOUR PROBLEMS WITH GRAHAM. WHY DON'T YOU TRY THE SAME TRICK I USED TO GET OFF WITH DENNIS? NOW, HERE'S WHAT I DID . . . BUT, REMEMBER, THIS IS JUST BETWEEN THE TWO OF US . . .

IT WAS NICE TO DREAM. BUT, A COUPLE OF WEEKS LATER . . .

I'VE HAD A REPLY FROM DOWNING STREET AND ONE FROM MOSCOW. THEY'RE NOT MUCH HELP, THOUGH. THE LETTERS HAVE BEEN WRITTEN BY THEIR SECRETARIES. THEY'RE VERY POLITE, BUT THEY JUST SAY THEY HOPE MY PROBLEM'LL SOON SORT ITSELF OUT.

JUST THEN . . .

HI. IS THIS MONTH'S PHILATELY MAGAZINE IN YET?

OH . . . EM . . . YES, I THINK SO. JUST A MINUTE AND I'LL GET IT FOR YOU.

I WISH I COULD THINK OF SOMETHING TO SAY TO HIM.

THANKS. OH, ARE THOSE YOUR LETTERS ON THE FLOOR? YOU MUST'VE KNOCKED THEM OFF THE COUNTER WHEN YOU WERE LOOKING FOR MY MAGAZINE.

OH, NO! I'D BETTER GRAB THEM BEFORE HE SEES WHAT THEY ARE. IT WOULD BE REALLY EMBARRASSING IF HE KNEW I'D BEEN WRITING TO THATCHER AND GORBACHEV ABOUT HIM!

BUT . . .

HEY, THIS ONE'S FROM RUSSIA. I RECOGNISE THE STAMP.

THAT'S RIGHT. I'VE — ER — GOT A PENPAL OVER THERE.

I DON'T SUPPOSE MR GORBACHEV WOULD MIND ME CALLING HIM THAT!

IT'S FROM THE LATEST SERIES OF RUSSIAN STAMPS THEY'VE JUST ISSUED. I HAVEN'T GOT THAT ONE YET.

THE POSTMARK'S MISSED THE STAMP, TOO. THAT MEANS IT'S STILL IN PERFECT CONDITION. I DON'T SUPPOSE I COULD HAVE IT, COULD I? IT WOULD BE GREAT FOR MY COLLECTION.

YEAH, SURE — YOU'RE WELCOME TO HAVE IT.

AND . . .

THAT'S GREAT. CAN I BUY YOU A COFFEE OR SOMETHING LATER TO SAY THANKS?

DEFINITELY! I MEAN, OK — THAT WOULD BE NICE.

AND . . .

I'VE BEEN WANTING TO GET TO KNOW YOU FOR QUITE A WHILE, SALLY. I NOTICED YOU EVERY TIME I CAME INTO THE SHOP, BUT I COULDN'T GET UP ENOUGH NERVE TO TALK TO YOU.

DID YOU, GRAHAM? I — I DIDN'T KNOW.

IT WAS LUCKY YOU GOT THAT LETTER FROM RUSSIA. IF YOU HADN'T, WE'D PROBABLY NEVER HAVE GOT TALKING . . .

HALF AN HOUR LATER . . .

I LIKE TALKING TO YOU, SALLY. NOT MANY GIRLS ARE INTERESTED IN HEARING ABOUT MY HOBBY.

I DON'T MIND, GRAHAM. I JUST LIKE LISTENING TO YOU TALK.

BUT, ANOTHER HOUR LATER . . .

. . . AND THEN THERE WAS THE ONE I MANAGED TO FIND LAST WEEK. A PERUVIAN BLUE. A LOT OF PEOPLE GET IT CONFUSED WITH THE PERUVIAN MAUVE, BUT THE BLUE HAS 32 PERFORATIONS AROUND THE EDGE OF THE STAMP AND THE MAUVE'S ONLY GOT 31.

BUT MY REAL AMBITION'S TO GET MY HANDS ON AN ALBANIAN 50 DINTAR STAMP. THAT'S FROM THE SERIES THAT WAS ISSUED IN 1968, OF COURSE, NOT THE 1966 ONES . . .

I'M NOT BORING YOU BY THE WAY, AM I?

MMM? OH, NO . . . I DON'T KNOW WHY YOU SHOULD THINK THAT, GRAHAM!

GOOD. ONCE I START TALKING ABOUT STAMPS, I CAN GO ON ALL NIGHT.

AND HE SOUNDS LIKE HE'S PLANNING TO! WHY DID I HAVE TO TELL HIM I LIKE LISTENING TO HIM TALK?

NEXT DAY . . .

I JUST DON'T KNOW HOW TO HANDLE THIS SITUATION. I NEED ADVICE. THERE'S ONLY ONE THING TO DO . . .

"DEAR PRIME MINISTER. YOU PROBABLY REMEMBER I WROTE TO YOU BEFORE, BUT I'VE GOT A MUCH WORSE PROBLEM NOW AND I REALLY NEED YOUR HELP . . . GRAHAM'S DRIVING ME MAD. PLEASE CAN YOU ADVISE ME OF THE BEST WAY TO GO ABOUT BREAKING OFF EAST-WEST RELATIONS . . ."

THE END

EVER FALLEN

SOME CASE HISTORIES

CATHY AND HEATHCLIFF

Perhaps the most classic example of love that should never have been is taken from Emily Bronte's novel, "Wuthering Heights". Cathy and Heathcliff — her father's adopted son — grew up together and loved each other madly. However, Cathy yearned for the life of a lady of leisure so, when her wealthy neighbour, Edgar Linton, proposed, she eventually accepted.

Heathcliff, on the other hand, had already realised that he would be unable to keep Cathy in the manner to which she aspired and had gone off to America (as you would!) to seek fame and fortune. When he returns to England and discovers that his childhood sweetheart is now the happily-married Mrs Cathy Linton, he winds up marrying Edgar's sister. The story would end here except that Heathcliff hears that Cathy is gravely ill and rushes to her bedside where they swear undying love for one another . . . then she dies! Heathcliff meets his untimely, but *welcome*, end soon afterwards while chasing Cathy's *ghost* in a blizzard. Poor soul!

LIZ TAYLOR AND RICHARD BURTON

It might seem like an odd combination, but for Hollywood's fieriest screen queen and Britain's booziest Hamlet, it was love at first sight on the set of "Cleopatra". Unfortunately, both of them were married at the time, but, as soon as their divorces were granted, they ran off and were wed.

Being two of the biggest names in the film industry obviously meant that they wouldn't have much privacy and, before long, there were rumours that their marriage was on the rocks. Soon afterwards, they divorced.

At this point, a strange thing happened. Burton began to shower Taylor with expensive gifts (including some of the world's biggest

shiny stones) and they gradually drifted back together. Once again, wedding bells were ringing for Rich and his gal.

After a short while, newspapers were regularly telling of feuds, fights and break-ups between the "Battling Burtons" and it seemed that although they couldn't live without each other, they certainly couldn't live *with* each other! A second divorce followed.

Both married others but friends claimed that they were still madly in love and, when Richard died in 1984, Elizabeth Taylor was there alongside his last wife Sally Burton and they comforted each other.

IN LOVE . . . ?

MARILYN MONROE AND NEARLY-EVERYONE-SHE-WENT-OUT-WITH!

Marilyn, although a great success on the big screen, wasn't too successful when it came to men. Whether this was due to her own insecurity or her choice of men is debatable, but, whatever the reason, she was infamous for being one half of a bad match!

When she was only 16, Norma Jean Baker married Jim Docherty but, when he joined the Marines at the outset of WWII and modelling contracts turned into offers from Hollywood, she said goodbye to her old self, her old name and her husband.

Husband No. 2 was top baseball player and living legend Joe Dimaggio. Unfortunately, Joe soon realised that Marilyn belonged not just to him, but to Hollywood. The final straw was when he saw Marilyn's skirt-blowing scene in "The Seven Year Itch". They divorced.

Her final marriage to playwright Arthur Miller, was an even stranger match — he was a quiet academic, quite the opposite of Marilyn — and it was destined to fail.

Marilyn's biggest mistake, however, was her much-publicised affair with the then president, John F. Kennedy. Her dream — for him to leave his wife, Jackie, and make Marilyn First Lady — would come to nothing because a scandal of that scale would have a devastating effect on his popularity. In the end, it had a devastating effect on Marilyn, who was found dead soon afterwards . . . and caused speculation over whether she died at her own hand, or at someone else's.

BARBRA STREISAND AND DON JOHNSON

These sneaky foxes managed to keep their relationship a secret but every time the news broke, so did the romance. However, the on-off, on-off, on-off pattern of their relationship came to an end when pictures of Don with his ex-wife regularly hit the news-stands; Barbra supposedly told him to give her 100% of her attention or nothing. He chose the latter!

Ms Streisand was said to be "inconsolable", especially when Don and his "floozie" got engaged. Well, he was too young for her anyway!

TOP TEN ROCKY ROMANCES

1. Brigitte Nielson and Sylvester Stallone
2. Madonna and Sean Penn
3. Rob Lowe and Melissa Gilbert
4. Prince and Sheena Easton
5. Cynthia and John Lennon
6. Ike and Tina Turner
7. 'Chelle and Lofty (EastEnders)
8. Joan Collins and Peter Holm
9. Charlene and Scott (Neighbours)
10. Maddie and David Addison (Moonlighting)

Why do some girls fall in love with someone totally wrong for them? It could be one of a few reasons.

* The Emotional Challenge. Just like men enjoy 'the chase', women get a kick out of conquering someone unsuitable then changing them into what they want them to be. Needless to say, they fail.
* They can't get anyone better — or so they think! Usually, their partners take advantage of their lack of self esteem so they don't stray.
* Physical attraction. They tend to ignore their partner's faults and concentrate on the fact that they're so lucky to be going out with someone like him.

But, whatever the reason, when a romance breaks down with Mr Wrong, it's quite likely to leave you more broken-hearted than if it had been Mr Right.

HOW TO AVOID MR WRONG

* Keep well away from the well-known 'man-about-town'. It's very unlikely that he's looking for a serious relationship.
* If he's someone else's — forget him. You don't want to get serious with someone who is prepared to two-time their partner. If he's really keen on you, he'll finish with them *first*.
* Take note of any 'feelings in your bones' — if there's something not quite right — stay put.
* Get to know him before you decide to go out with him. Talk to him, and if he genuinely seems nice, take the chance. If you're in doubt — don't!
* Ask your friends about him. If he's got a bad reputation you'll soon find out about it. Take note of people's reactions when you ask them about him.

HOW TO GET OVER HIM

So, the sad inevitable has happened — it's over. It's no use letting all the sadness and disappointment drain you — you're to think positive and get on with life. Follow The Jackie Guide to Getting Him Out of Your System, and weather the storm.
* Have a good cry. Remember all the bad things about him and what he's done to you, then have a good cry again.
* Tell a good friend what's happened. You don't have to talk about it in full yet, just tell her to inform those who need to know so you don't have to face up to questions like, "Oh, hi! How's Tony these days?"
* Put everything he's ever given you in a box and stash it in the loft/cellar/garage so you're not continually reminded of him. If it makes you feel any better, ceremoniously burn them.
* Depending on the type of person you are and how out of touch with your friends you are, move back gently into the social whirl. If you're still too upset to face anyone, have a few friends over but if you're brave, go out and live it up.
* If you see him, don't run into the nearest shop. Face him. If you can't bring yourself to speak to him just ignore him. If you can, just say hello. You might feel a surge of regret and depression, but remember all those horrible things he's done to you and you'll feel stronger.

After you feel better about everything, remembering the good times shouldn't feel so painful.

SMART MEN
JACKIE TAKES A QUICK LOOK AT THE REAL SMOOTHY MEN OF OUR SCREENS IN ALL THEIR STYLISH SPLENDOUR . . .

TOM JONES wouldn't be seen dead without his smoothy-smart polo-neck. What's that you say? No, of course he doesn't wear it to cover his wrinkles!

MICK HUCKNALL: If we chop off his head, poor ol' Mick *could* be mistaken for a smoothie. But with that awful mop nestling on his head, well . . .

BROS sit back and ponder how wonderful they are for looking spruce without looking stuffy.

RICK ASTLEY: Now here's one boy your Mum would love you to bring home for tea — even if you wouldn't!

JONATHAN WOSS (sorry 'Ross') looks just wovely in his many a wardrobe full of pinstwipes!

BRYAN FERRY: Aah! Smooth, smart, sophisticated and just a mite saucy; a gentleman indeedy!

PHILLIP SCHOFIELD, JASON CONNERY and **MATTHEW BRODERICK** have a lot in common — they all like to p-p-pick up a penguin suit before watching the birdie!

SLOB MEN

SOME TRY AND FAIL AT THE FASHION STAKES, BUT MOST OF THE FOLLOWING ARE JUST NATURALLY BORN SLOBS . . .

BOB GELDOF: "Oh, if only I could get my hands on some soap and a razor!"

BRUCE SPRINGSTEEN earns a few quid busking — he doesn't get paid overly much as a garage mechanic, you know!

PHIL COLLINS often sports the back-combed look, or is it the just-rolled-out-of-bed look?

BRUCE WILLIS obviously still thinks he's playing the part of Moonlighting detective, David Addison. Here he's cleverly disguised so as to merge in with a very dirty room.

MICKEY ROURKE
The type of s
you smell
before you s

ERASURE like to make their fans feel at ease by wearing the "I've-just-come-in-from-walking-the-dog" look. Vincent has also worked out a way to avoid the tedious task of washing his hair.

DAVE STEWART has to wear sunglasses all the year round to cut down the dazzling effects of his dandruff.

IAN GILLAN explains to the world how to become a perfect slob by cutting the arms off all upper clothing and rebelling against that 'every 6-8 weeks trim to get rid of split ends' rule.

STING makes thousands homeless when he swings his mane of hair (!) — and it looks like his underarm deodorant's beginning to wear off . . .

41

A KICK UP THE 80'S

What moment from the last ten years do you cherish most? What would you rather forget about? Who or what made the 80's a "happening" time for you?

We took these questions out onto the streets and hurled them at unsuspecting passers-by . . .

Margaret (15)

"Oh, the 80's were just fabulous. There was always something going on to make life interesting. Curiosity Killed The Cat were all right and T'Pau were another band I liked a lot. The breakdancing craze was quite fun, but absolutely *nothing* could compare to the main event of the '80's . . . 'Brookside'! I never miss an episode. Never!

"Oh, Mel Gibson was kinda cute as well!"

Alison (18)

"The best thing that happened to me in the 80's was leaving school. Once I got all my qualifications I couldn't wait to get out. Possibly the worst thing I've seen fashion-wise were 'Moon boots' — they were really terrible. The best thing in the movies was Tom Cruise — I'll bet he increased cinema attendance!"

Roddy Frame (Aztec Camera)

Roddy's most hated TV programme of the 80's was "Blind Date".

"I got Cilla's autograph when I saw her in Blackpool once. She was dead nice . . . terrible programme, though! Pure cringe value!"

One of the worst moments of the 80's for Roddy was when Hilda Ogden left "Coronation Street".

"The programme is over as far as I'm concerned!"

42

Gillian (13) ▲

"The return of 'flares' I think I could've done without, even if they *weren't* back for very long! Anything in tartan was really horrible, too. Levi 501's are superb, though!"

And what were the big hits of the 80's for her?

"Definitely Rick Astley and 'Neighbours'! I don't think I could get by without either of them."

Diane (19)

"I liked bands like Deacon Blue but all that Acid House stuff passed me by, fortunately. Spandau Ballet were good right at the beginning and, I'm sorry if anyone has already said that Levi 501's were the best in fashion, but they were!"

Shona (18) ▶

"Tight jeans were probably the biggest turn-off for me in the Eighties . . . give me baggy trousers any day! As far as music goes, Kylie Minogue and Tiffany were pretty good and some of the House stuff that was around was great. It's also good to see lots of Australian programmes on TV. I was there recently and it's just wonderful!"

Arlene (14) ▲

"Lots of horrible things happened in the 80's, all sorts of disasters and things, but lots of nice things, too. I went to Spain on holiday(!), which was good . . . and Steve Beattie came into Gillian's life!"

(Big blushes from Gillian, accompanied by a playful punch in the shoulder!)

"It's good that more people started wearing hats as well and, as for telly, well, "EastEnders" is my kind of soap."

Ann (17) ▼

"For a start, I think late night telly is the best idea for a long time, though it does give you a hard time getting up in the morning. Wet Wet Wet and New Order were the best bands of the 80's!"

Jackie (18)

"The 80's were quite good to me — I passed my driving test, for a start! Other good things about them were the fashions — when they were good they were really good, but when they were bad they were just awful — all those white stilettos people were wearing to nightclubs. Yuk!

"The best thing on TV was 'Bread' and 'The Chart Show' was quite good as well. Matt Goss was the most kissable man to come out of the 80's!"

Nicky (17) ▼

"I think the Live Aid and Comic Relief Concerts were brilliant and there were some great films about too, like "Shag" and "Pretty In Pink" — Andrew McCarthy is something else!"

43

TURNING THE TABLES!

"I'M THE QUIET TYPE — TOO QUIET FOR MY OWN GOOD, I SOMETIMES THINK. UNLIKE MY SISTER, TRACEY . . ."

SUE — CAN I BORROW YOUR NEW TOP TONIGHT? I'M GOING TO ANOTHER PARTY.

NO, YOU CAN'T. I'M FED UP WITH YOU BORROWING MY STUFF — AND, ANYWAY, I WANT TO WEAR IT MYSELF TONIGHT.

HA! THAT'S A LAUGH! GOING TO WATCH TV IN IT, OR SOMETHING?

SHE'S RIGHT, I SUPPOSE. I'M NOT GOING ANYWHERE, AS USUAL. SHE MAY AS WELL TAKE IT . . .

"MY KID BROTHER, GREG, THINKS I'M SOFT IN THE HEAD, TOO . . ."

HEY, SIS. I'M DOING A SPONSORED SILENCE AT SCHOOL, SO I'VE PUT YOU DOWN FOR FIFTY PENCE, OK?

WELL, I'M HARDLY LIKELY TO LOSE ANY MONEY, AM I? YOU COULD HAVE ASKED ME FIRST, THOUGH . . .

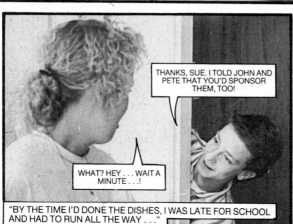

THANKS, SUE. I TOLD JOHN AND PETE THAT YOU'D SPONSOR THEM, TOO!

WHAT? HEY . . . WAIT A MINUTE . . .!

"BY THE TIME I'D DONE THE DISHES, I WAS LATE FOR SCHOOL AND HAD TO RUN ALL THE WAY . . ."

"AND, AT SCHOOL, THERE WAS ANOTHER PROBLEM I HAD TO PUT UP WITH . . ."

WELL, WELL. IF IT ISN'T THE SCARECROW! DRAG YOURSELF THROUGH A HEDGE ON YOUR WAY TO SCHOOL, DID YOU?

I WISH BECKY'D LEAVE OFF. I'M FED UP WITH HER PICKING ON THE WAY I DRESS AND EVERYTHING. BUT I JUST CAN'T THINK OF ANYTHING SMART TO SAY TO SHUT HER UP . . .

"WHEN I FINALLY GOT HOME . . ."

THANK GOODNESS — THE END OF ANOTHER ROTTEN DAY. I THINK I'LL GO DOWN TO THE DISCO TONIGHT. MAYBE I'LL BE LUCKY AND SEE ROB JACKSON THERE! I MUST FIND THAT TOP TRACEY BORROWED, THOUGH . . .

"AS I WAS GOING UP TO MY ROOM, GREG AND HIS HORRIBLE LITTLE FRIENDS CAME CHARGING DOWN THE STAIRS . . ."

D'YOU RECKON YOU COULD BE A BIT MORE CAREFUL, YOU LITTLE HORRORS? I'M ALLOWED TO USE THESE STAIRS TOO, Y'KNOW.

SORRY, SIS. C'MON LADS, LET'S GET OUT OF HERE QUICK!

HMM . . . WHAT HAVE THEY BEEN UP TO, I WONDER . . .?

"I SHOULD'VE KNOWN . . ."

I — I'LL KILL THEM! WHAT A MESS! THEY — THEY'VE THROWN ALL MY STUFF AROUND!

"ONCE I'D SORTED THE MESS OUT, I LOOKED FOR THE TOP THAT TRACEY'D BORROWED . . ."

I DON'T BELIEVE IT! HOW COULD SHE LEAVE IT IN SUCH A MESS? SHE HASN'T EVEN WASHED IT! OH, WELL, I SUPPOSE I'LL HAVE TO WEAR MY USUAL RED TOP . . . AT LEAST KEVIN'S DOING THE DISHES TONIGHT, SO I'LL GET TO THE DISCO ON TIME . . .

"BUT I SHOULD'VE KNOWN BETTER . . ."

OK, THEN, THAT'S ME AWAY. I'LL SEE YOU LATER . . .

BUT — BUT IT'S YOUR TURN TO DO THE DISHES. YOU PROMISED!

WHAT? OH, YEAH, THAT'S RIGHT. WELL, YOU CAN DO THEM JUST THIS ONCE, THEN . . .

"NEEDLESS TO SAY . . ."

WHY ME? WHY DO I LET HIM TALK ME INTO DOING HIS WORK FOR HIM? NOW I'LL BE LATE FOR THE DISCO . . .

"HOWEVER, WHEN I FINALLY GOT THERE, THE MOST BRILLIANT THING HAPPENED . . ."

HI, SUE. I SAW YOU COME IN. D'YOU WANT TO DANCE?

WH-WHAT? ER, YES . . . I'D LOVE TO, ROB!

"BUT . . ."

HELLO, SUE — I THOUGHT I SMELT MOTHBALLS! ISN'T IT ABOUT TIME YOU BURNT THAT RELIC YOU'RE WEARING?

OH, NO! HOW EMBARRASSING — AND IN FRONT OF ROB, TOO. HE'LL NEVER SPEAK TO ME AGAIN . . .

"I MADE SOME EXCUSE AND DASHED OFF . . ."

I WAS PATHETIC IN THERE. I JUST LET HER EMBARRASS ME WITHOUT SAYING ONE WORD IN DEFENCE. WELL, I'VE HAD ENOUGH!

"I DECIDED THAT I, SUE GREEN, WAS GOING TO FIGHT BACK . . ."

"SO, NEXT MORNING . . ."

RIGHT, THAT'S ALL OF TRACEY'S JUNK OUT OF MY ROOM AND INTO THE BIN, AND THIS LOT'S THE STUFF SHE'S BORROWED AND HASN'T BOTHERED CLEANING. HUH! I'LL SOON SORT THAT!

"SO, IT WAS A TRIP TO THE LAUNDRETTE . . ."

NOW THAT'S EVERYTHING WASHED AND DRIED. I'LL GET A BILL MADE OUT TO TRACEY FOR THE MONEY I'VE SPENT . . .

"AND, NEXT MORNING . . ."

D'YOU MIND TELLING ME WHAT THIS BILL IS ALL ABOUT?

OF COURSE. IT'S A BILL FOR ALL MY CLOTHES THAT YOU MUCKED UP AND DIDN'T BOTHER WASHING. OH, AND YOUR JUNK IS IN THE BIN, SO IF YOU WANT IT BACK, YOU'D BETTER HURRY — THE DUSTMEN'LL BE HERE SOON!

"KEV WAS NEXT. SO, THAT EVENING, WHEN HE WAS IN WITH HIS GIRLFRIEND . . ."

HI, EMMA. OH, BY THE WAY, KEV, YOU KNOW JOYCE? THAT BLONDE FROM THE CHIP SHOP? WELL, SHE PHONED AND SAID THANKS FOR THE OFFER AND SHE'LL MEET YOU WHEN SHE'S FINISHED WORK!

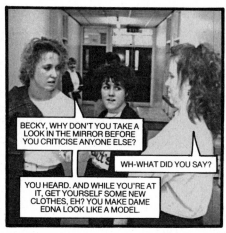

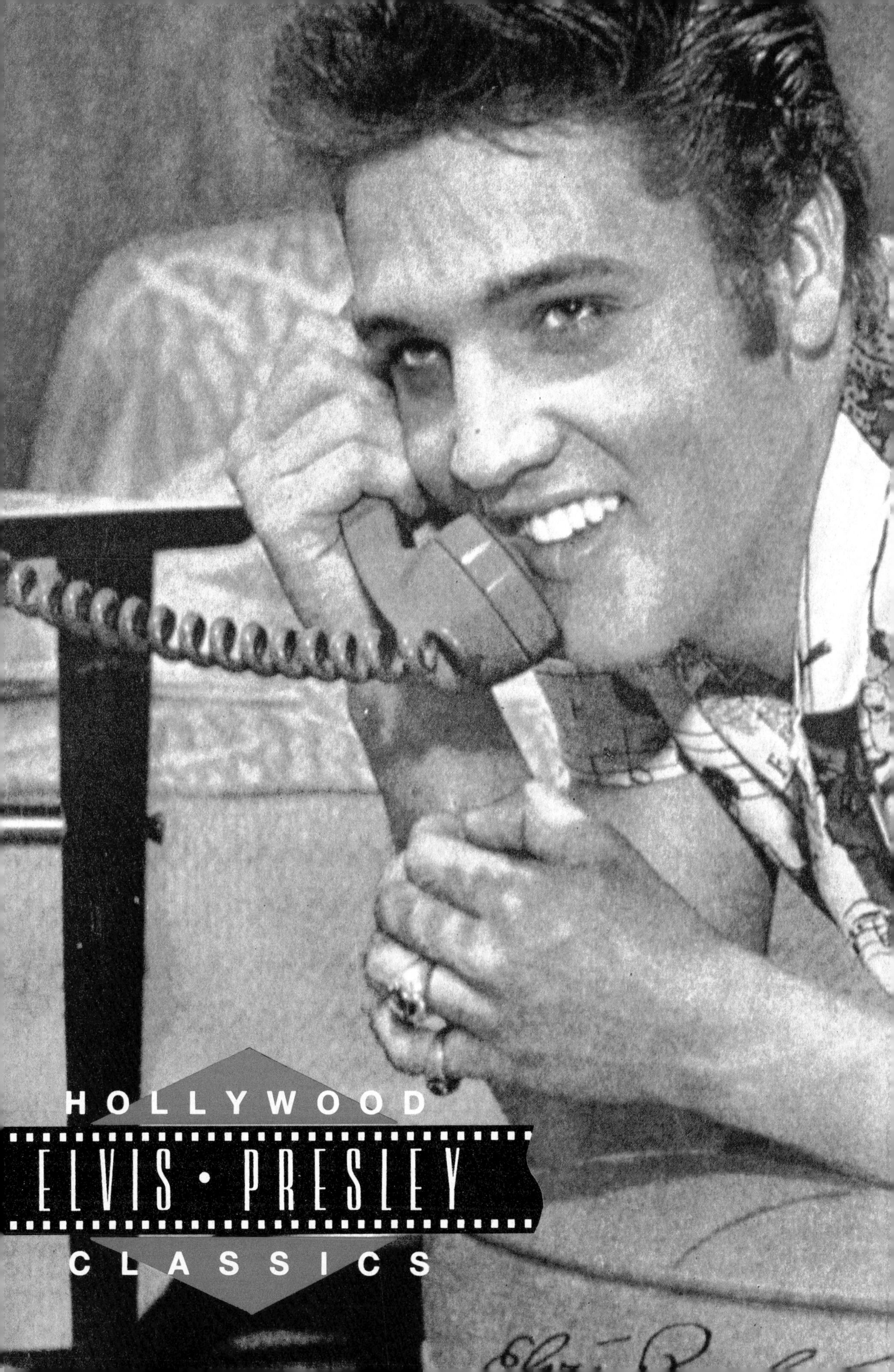
HOLLYWOOD
ELVIS • PRESLEY
CLASSICS

A NEW SENSATION

FIRST KISS

THE first kiss is usually dreaded. Questions such as will our teeth clash, does my breath smell, who should make the first move, rush through our minds when we think a pucker-up session's soon to come. In fact, the first kiss seems so nerve-wracking a thought we start wanting it to just be over and done with, which spoils the whole thing! Of course, we can't tell you how to kiss — it's highly personal and the technique comes naturally — but you can follow certain rules for kissing confidence. Try to brush your teeth at least twice a day and after meals if possible. If you can't brush your teeth after you've eaten, wash your mouth out with water to get rid of any smelly bacteria lurking about. If you're a bad breath victim, swill your mouth out at morning and night with a minty gargle. Stay clear of strong foods, such as garlic and onions, and drink plenty of water — even carry a breath freshener. If you have persistent bad breath, though, go for a check-up at the dentist — there may be a medical reason.

For those of you who have to wear a brace, and feel conscious about Mr Lush coming into contact with a mouthful of metal, you could always take it out for such a special occasion!

Right, now we've got the bad breath and brace worry over, let's discuss the actual kiss. Lots of terms are used to describe this passion action such as a tongue-sarnie, French kissing and snogging. Don't think these terms mean you need a degree to have a successful kiss.

A kiss can be light and friendly or deep and meaningful. It can be a quick peck on the lips or the more intimate type of French (or tongue) kissing. It's probably best to save this for when you really know and trust the boy you're seeing.

Kisses can't be planned though, they happen spontaneously when the mood and moment's right. This means your lips could meet in the disco during your first date or a few weeks later when you both feel confident enough to start building up a relationship together.

Feeling easy in each other's company is often enough to spark off a brilliant kiss! Just make sure you don't let trivial things come between you. For instance, who cares if you're taller or shorter than your boyfriend? When it comes to kissing, it only makes it more fun to find a way round it! The same goes if you both sport specs.

And remember, even if your teeth do crunch together or something else goes disastrously wrong, just laugh and try again. Kissing isn't an exam; it's designed to show the other person you fancy them and give you both a lovely warm glow! So don't pay too much attention to the kissing routine — until it actually happens! ●

FIRST DATE

YOUR first date, whether going to a disco, to the pictures or just for a walk, doesn't need to be a harrowing experience — though it can't be denied when you meet that boy you fancy outside of the usual school surroundings and, worse, all on your ownsome, it's enough to make the most super-cool girl wibble with nerves.

The trick for success is to relax. Remind yourself that he already likes you or he wouldn't have asked you out. Don't feel you have to suddenly whitter on wittily just because you're out on a date. The same goes for your make-up — avoid going overboard on it. If he's used to seeing you fresh-faced and clean-cut, it could frighten him off if he suddenly sees you three eyeliners and two tubes of foundation later. Subtlety's the key. In fact, as an alternative to gooey lipstick, for instance, try using lip balm — it won't dehydrate your lips, leaving them dry and sore (not so good for kissing anyway!). Lipstick also has the disadvantage of getting all over his face, if the opportunity arises!

On the subject of kissing, don't feel that this is an essential part of your first date. It will happen when you both feel relaxed enough to let it, so don't worry. A thank-you peck on the lips from you at the end of the evening might be a nice idea though, to show you care!

Get ready for your date in plenty of time but not hours earlier than necessary or you'll feel exhausted even before you step outside! Have a bath or shower and wash and style your hair to, hopefully, relax and refresh you. Try to find out where you'll be off to on your date — that skimpy black dress and stilletos may look a bit out of place for a walk in the park! More importantly, though, always wear something you feel comfortable in and again, wherever you're going, don't go over the top or you'll find yourself constantly worrying about your appearance, such as whether the seams in your stockings are straight.

Who pays on your first date doesn't need to cause a headache. If possible, always offer to pay your own way then things are equal from the start.

Going to the pictures is an easy first date as there won't

It's not all fun being a teenager, is it? It can be frightening not knowing how to cope with situations you've never been through before. Well, help is at hand! Here we explore everything from dealing with that first kiss to preparing for college — and much more inbetween!

FIRST CRUSH

A CRUSH can be very painful and often you can be convinced that it's real love. If you find yourself snipping out every picture you can find of a certain pop star and sticking them on your bedroom wall, watch out! It's nice to have someone to occasionally fantasise about, but be careful it doesn't turn into an obsession. You can tell when this happens because you'll prefer to sit at home and listen to HIS records and look at HIS pictures than going out with people your own age. You'll begin to compare boys you know to your idol and they might seem so young you can't be bothered with them. This is when a crush can be dangerous. You won't be able to concentrate on your schoolwork or you'll neglect your friends — you'll be too busy day-dreaming about what it will be like when fate brings you and Mr Fantasy together to bother with reality . . . If you can't get over this infatuation, you're going to end up being very lonely.

A crush is a phase which most girls go through in their pre-boyfriend years. It's a rehearsal for the real thing which they're not quite ready to handle. In a way, it's an attempt to fill a gap in their life and the only cure is to remember that your idol is no better than that boy in your class, for example. Nobody is perfect. Take down some of those pictures, put away his records for a while (if he's a pop star) and start to involve yourself in real people's lives again. Soon, you'll have no need to create little fantasies

for yourself as you meet new and interesting people to spend time with instead.

The above is the unrequited type of crush when all the floods of feelings are directed to a star who might as well be in another galaxy! The other, more realistic, kind can be on the boy next door, the boy who sits opposite you in class or the boy you pass every morning as he walks his dog. Whoever he is, chances are you've not spoken to him much, if at all. Maybe you've 'progressed' enough to squirm and squeal "hello" when you see him but not much else.

It may be that this boy is more accessible, so it's worth giving it your best to see if he's interested. Force yourself to start a conversation and take it from there. Soon, you should be honest with yourself and ask yourself if he feels the same. If not, put things into

perspective, go back to just smiling and saying hello and look for somebody else.

Both types of crushes can be very painful and feel like true love because you know no better. Possibly more hurtful is being told forty-twelve times "It's only a crush", even if it is! Just try to accept it gracefully as a phase of growing up that we all have to go through and learn from it, enjoy it even, without wallowing in it, while it lasts. ●

FIRST HEARTBREAK

IT'S always a blow when suddenly you're no longer with that person who you were so close to, that boy who was not only a boyfriend but your best friend. Suddenly you split up. Of course, if this was your choice it will be easier to cope with — you're bound to miss him occasionally and maybe feel a sense of guilt. But if he caused the break-up, it can seem shattering. Firstly you'll mope, cry and even feel that your life is empty now he's gone.

Whatever you do, don't write or phone, begging for him to come back. After he's refused, you'll only end up feeling as if you've lost all your pride.

Of course, it's natural to feel a great sense of loss to begin with. It's likely to be red eyes and blotchy skin for a while but don't allow yourself to be dragged down in self-pity for too long. There comes a point when you'll have to stop crying over his letters, cards and constantly

listening to 'your songs'. For once, maybe you should listen to those who love you and try to "pull yourself together". One of the world's most popular philosophers believed you could actually choose your own mood — so try this approach.

If the only way you feel you can help yourself get over it is to feel angry with him by asking yourself, "Who does he think he is to chuck me?" and concentrate on some of his bad points, then that's a good starting point.

Pour out all your feelings to someone who will sympathise with you, who'll agree that you were too good for him, who always thought he was a rat etc., etc. Let this be your last moping session though. People, even best friends, will get sick of you if you go on for too long. Start to rebuild your life — you'll probably realise that far too much of your time was devoted to one person, anyway. It's time to indulge yourself by doing all those

things you've always fancied, whether it's going to karate classes, buying those Doc Marten's, or getting that short crop you've always fancied but knew he wouldn't approve of! Involve yourself in your friends' activities again — you'll be surprised how much you've been missing out on.

You'll probably meet up with him sooner or later and this could be a sticky situation. Even if you parted agreeing to remain friends, it's easier said than done. Don't make the mistake of ignoring him — it shows you're bothered about him. Instead, scrunch your courage together, smile, say hello and walk on. This way, you won't have enough time for the waterworks to start but at the same time it shows him you're coping on your own.

Chances are you'll wonder why you made such a fuss over him in the first place! ●

be much opportunity to get tongue-tied and the film will give you something to chat about if you go for a coffee after it. Don't worry about lapses in conversation or feel embarrassed every time there's a silence as you'll only be completely stuck for something sparkling to say! On the other hand, don't blab on about your favourite things all night long in case it's not his cup of tea. Try to find out what makes him tick by asking him about himself — he'll be flattered you're so bothered about his life.

But above all, relax — and things should go silky-smooth! ●

A NEW SENSATION

FIRST PERIOD

SOME girls dread it, some look forward to it and find it a relief when it starts; but, like it or not, having periods is just another natural part of growing up, like developing curves and noticing boys.

They can start when you're as young as 9 or as mature as 18, but about 13's the average age.

Having a period, or menstruating, is sometimes referred to as having a 'monthly' which is misleading as it's more common *not* to have a cycle as regular as clock-work, especially for the first few years.

It takes time for your hormones to adjust to the physical upheaval your body's going through right now, which is why there might be a gap of months between your first and second period.

When some sort of pattern's been established, periods will span around 3-8 days and can sometimes be cut short by factors such as serious illness, dieting and worry.

What basically happens during a period, as you probably already know (unless you haven't been paying attention in biology class!), is that your sex hormones cause thousands of tiny egg cells (or ovum) to ripen, of which one or two each month will be released and passed, in 2-5 days, through one of the Fallopian tubes into the womb (uterus). Ready to hold it, the uterus wall thickens and richens with blood. Here, the cell settles and a baby grows from it if the egg has been fertilised through sexual intercourse; if not, it breaks up. A period isn't this miniscule cell being expelled but the, by now unneeded, uterus lining. The actual blood loss will seem heavier than the couple of tablespoons it really is.

Especially if you have irregular periods, the whole process can cause mild aches and pains or nasty cramps — which is how that old-fashioned (and awful) descriptive nickname of 'the curse' came about! The discomfort will probably make you want to curl up and rest, but the best pain-reliever is actually exercise, to gently

FIRST MAKE-UP

WHEN it comes to putting on make-up, practice really does make perfect. There's lots of skills to get used to, such as matching foundation to skin colour and type and how to apply eyeliner without poking your eyes out!

The trick is to become familiar with your own features, enhancing the best ones and playing down the not-so-hot. Buy or borrow a good up-to-date beauty book to inform you on defining and applying make-up to suit your particular facial characteristics — like a long face, square jaw, prominent eyes or snub nose.

Then study the beauty pages in magazines (such as Jackie!) for ideas and have fun playing at beauticians with a friend! Build up a box of colours together too, to make your make-up stretch twice as far (but splash out on your own foundation and

ease out your stomach muscles. If you really can't face stretching, a warm bath and holding a hot water bottle will help — as well as an aspirin, a Feminax tablet or homeopathic preparation from any health food store.

If your period hasn't started yet, don't worry that at school it'll catch you out with a big rush of blood. Usually, you'll notice a few days beforehand slight spotting or a coloured discharge. When this happens, prepare yourself by popping a couple of sanitary

towels in your bag. If you feel comfortable about using these permanently, that's fine; but you might find tampons more convenient and after a bit of practice you'll find them really easy to insert. They always come with instructions and useful addresses you can write to if you need sensible advice.

Speaking of which, confiding in your mum could well help. Don't be embarrassed — after all, she's been having the same experience for years! ●

powder as your skin types probably won't be the same).

Experiment with different colours and ways of applying them to find effects which suit you most or look best for day or evening.

Don't make the mistake of drowning your face in a sea of colour — you're supposed to show off your beauty not layers of products! Aim for subtlety.

The way you apply cosmetics and the equipment you use makes a big difference to the end result. Make sure your skin's clean before you start. Use cleanser with cotton-wool if you find soap and water drying, then tone to tighten pores and moisturise. Cover any spots or dark eye circles with concealer. In a shade matching your skin tone, dab on foundation with a wedge of sponge, leaving no naff mark between face and neck! To prevent any shine and to set the foundation, dust on matching loose powder with a big, soft brush to whisk away any excess at the same time. Suck in cheeks to brush on powder blusher in a pinky shade if you're pale or coral if you're darker-skinned.

Eyes next! Stroke a light shade over the whole lid as a base. Top up with other colours or leave it natural. Mascara down the top side of upper lashes, go upwards and underneath them then fill in lower ones. Avoid harsh black unless your colouring's dark enough to take it. A toothbrush comes in handy to separate lashes and tidy brows. For slick lips, outline and fill in with a lipbrush; blot with a tissue. Reds compliment pouty mouths and gleaming pearly-whites; pinks and russets enlarge thin lips and brighten ivory teeth.

Like finding your own clothes style, it'll take you a while to create great make-up looks — but at least you can enjoy yourself finding out! ●

FIRST TIME
BEING BULLIED

BEING pushed around by a gang at school, a teacher constantly picking on you or a threatening boyfriend — can seem like a nightmare. But it's up to you to make the first time it happens the last. Whether this hassle makes you feel miserable or so scared you start missing school, keeping quiet about it is really the worst thing to do. Tell someone you can trust, like your parents or a teacher, exactly what's going on. It isn't telling tales, it's sensibly asking for help when you need it!

Also try to figure out why you're the target for the bullying. Maybe something you're doing accidentally, or intentionally, provokes it. For instance, if you come way down a certain teacher's favourite pupil list, ask yourself why. In class are you loud, rude or always handing work in late? If neither your attitude nor your work's really to blame, then maybe you both just clash — if so, explain your feelings to a sympathetic teacher. This can't make things worse, in one way or another it'll cause changes for the better, resulting in a class transfer or the picky teacher being at least more understanding.

If it's a school gang giving you a hard time, analyse the reasons why. You can't blame them hurling 'swot-face!' at you if your break-times are spent playing about with the square root of Pi instead of making an effort to join in! If the insult's more personal, ie — relating to the way you look, then simply ignore it. It's not a cop-out, it's the most effective reaction in the long run. Shouting names back will only encourage them; if they get no response, sooner or later they'll get bored and stop.

However, if the bullying is in any way physical, whether you've bruises or not to prove it, speak up. This is pure violence and totally unjustified. Ignore any blackmail about how heavy they'll get if you tell. Tell someone in authority and quick. You'll be surprised how soon this scares the bullies away from *you*.

Perhaps the most psychologically worst form of bullying is entangled with love — when the bully's a boy you're dating. Any sign of physical aggression he shows like slapping you during an argument or worse, take as a warning to leave the relationship — fast. Even if he's sweet and apologetic afterwards, usually if he's hit you once, he'll do it again — and the feelings of love you think you have for him now will rapidly turn into hate, distrust and fear. You're not that stupid to stick around that long, though, are you? If he keeps pestering you, get a beefy big brother, relation or dad to help you out.

Remember, to conquer the effect physical bullying has of making you feel alone, you need outside help to handle it. Being this kind of victim makes you feel weak and defenceless — a wimp, even; but you're only a wimp if you let yourself suffer in silence. ●

FIRST BEREAVEMENT

IF someone close to you *suddenly dies, it'll probably be the worst experience you'll ever have to face. The first time this happens will be especially painful as you won't have had any experience of how to cope. Losing someone means you'll naturally feel life's never going to be the same again and that it's impossible for you to ever be happy.*

We won't pretend such a trauma's easy to get over — it isn't. But, hard though it seems at the time, the hurt will gradually fade — and there are ways you can help this process along.

At first, of course, you'll feel nothing because the loss will seem too awful to be true. At some point, its impact will hit you and you'll experience feelings of shock, despair, misery and maybe anger, too. Whatever you feel, don't be afraid to cry. The worst thing to do is to try and deny your emotions. By releasing them, you're taking that first important step towards

facing up to your loss — and eventually healing your feelings. Go ahead and think of all the good memories you have and mourn all you want to.

Friends and family will probably want to help and console you, so let them. Organisations set up especially for bereaved people are also a great help because everyone there knows from experience what it's like to lose someone. Try contacting Cruse — Bereavement Care, at Cruse House, 126 Sheen Road, Richmond, Surrey TW9 1VR

for details of any self-help groups near you. It'll be of some relief just telling someone caring how you feel.

There's no set time for how long it takes to get over a death. It's far too personal to apply rules to. What might help, however, is to try and lose yourself in routine things, once you feel in control enough not to break down in public. This won't help you forget — at first it'll take raw courage to even attempt because you'll be reminded of that person constantly. Gradually, though, just being occupied will help take your mind off what's happened. Just think positively that the pain will lessen as time goes by — because the event will lose its freshness once other experiences good, bad, happy and sad have had the chance to happen. There'll always be times you'll miss that special person badly, but slowly, very slowly, you'll one day remember them — and smile. ●

A NEW SENSATION

FIRST TIME COLLEGE

COLLEGE can be the perfect place to broaden your mind, mix with loads of young people from all backgrounds and, by providing you with important qualifications, boost your chances of finding a good job. Or, it can be where you live like a pig, be a dirty stop-out, learn nothing and end up skint! The choice is yours.

If starting college also means a move to another town, it'll seem like Freedom City. You'll probably feel a mixture of excitement and butterflies at the thought of it.

For maybe the first time in your life, you'll be totally self-dependent and, strangely enough, probably homesick, too! This is especially true if you generally treat your mum like your slave. If this has been the case, don't go flat-sharing when you're not self-sufficient enough to handle it. Cooking, cleaning, just living with people you don't know, could be more of a nightmare than a dream if you're an only child whose idea of being domestic is to get your own cornflakes!

Until you feel you can cope, go for a half-way move instead into the college's Halls of Residence, which will soften the blow of being away from home — and not be quite as free and easy as a flat.

Something else you'll have to deal with is money in the form of a student grant. Don't be fooled into thinking you've hit the jackpot, this has to last a full term! If you've been used to splurging pocket money like there's no tomorrow, it could be difficult to master budgeting. Here's where banks come in handy with useful advice — and offers of 'easy money' credit cards! With their 'buy now, pay later' basis, they encourage impulse buying so, before you know it, you could well be sky-high in debt. As a student, make money your only currency then you'll have a realistic view of your financial affairs. Remember your grant's a means of support, not cash for trendy new clothes/cosmetics/records! Deposit the dosh in an account and generally take out a set amount each week.

What will really test your common sense/self-control at college, is the work itself. Unlike school-teachers, you won't get hassle from lecturers over late essays or your attendance, even. The reason being, the onus has shifted to you because you're

FIRST INTERVIEW

THE thought of attending an interview is as appealing as a trip to the dentist's, isn't it? Especially when you haven't been to one before. But there's not that much to it — honest! It just needs a bit of forward planning, that's all. Find out exactly where to go, how to get there and how far it is away. Also find out about the firm. If it's local, ask around or at the Careers Office or Job Centre if that's where the job was advertised. A bit of background information will boost your confidence and lessen chances of you — horrors! — drying up at the actual interview. It'll also show how enthusiastic you are. As useful practice, you could give yourself a mock interview with your mum or a friend acting as the interviewer.

Next, make a list of why you'd be great for the job — come on, don't be shy! Scribble things down like your keenness, willingness, etc., as well as qualities connected to the job you're after, such as getting on with people, good with money, if it's a record-shop assistant position, for instance.

Get the interview date and time imprinted on your brain. Don't be late and work out what to wear the night before. Unless you know in advance that anything goes, dressing to impress the interviewer doesn't mean thigh-high minis. But you don't have to go looking like a pensioner, either! Smart suits or separates that fit and flatter you are your best bet.

Don't forget to take the following with you to the interview — a note of the name, address and phone number of the firm and your interviewer's name; certificates or letters of reference you may have, any info sent to you before the interview and cash for travel fares and a phone call to the firm if you're held up en route.

Now for the wibbly-making bit — except it doesn't need to be! THE INTERVIEW ITSELF! Firstly, don't think of the interviewer as some kind of monster; they're there to give you the chance to see if you're the best one for the job so they'll generally want you to feel comfortable. Really sell yourself. Be friendly, interested and ask relevant questions. Expect to be asked why the job interests you, about your training, experience, hobbies, health and so on. Listen carefully and show you've got a bit up top — give more than 'yes' or 'no' answers!

Go on, show them what you're made of and good luck! And remember, if you don't get the job, it wasn't right for you in the first place! ●

no school-kid anymore! With all that's going on around you, it's easy to get caught up in the whirl of extra-curricular activity and neglect what you're there to do in the first place — work!

Never resort to cramming in revision the week before exams. A little often is the best bet for exam success. Get used to doing some work on a nightly basis, to make it seem familiar and less of a dreadful prospect. If you find it tough, speak up. Your lecturer will be only too pleased to help. Don't feel, though, that every spare minute is to be spent swotting! Aim for a balance. Find out what's going on socially and take the plunge — there's sure to be some party, disco, society or class to take your fancy! There'll also be heaps of boys competing for your attention, too! Resist going mad over all of them, though! A string of one-night stands isn't much fun. Neither is peer pressure — you could well see drugs passed around and feel tempted to join in to 'be in with the crowd'. Like everything with college, you'll have to use your common sense. It's all a great learning experience and can be the best time of your life — if you let it. ●

A FIRST party usually consists of weeks of planning — make-up, hair and more importantly, what to wear. You'll probably look forward to it so much that it's almost impossible for a party to reach your expectations! You'll spend literally hours getting ready, be quite pleased with the slinky reflection in the mirror then, once ensconced at the party, think everyone else looks miles better ...

The main thing to remember when preparing for a party is to wear something you feel comfortable in which won't cramp your dancing style! So disregard the skin-tight skirt and spike heels! If you don't want to stand out from the crowd too much, try to find out exactly what kind of party it is and what other people will be wearing, then you won't look snoot when everyone else is in jeans!

Also, ask whoever invited you who else is going. There should be somebody you know. If so, try and arrange to go with them. Nothing's more cringesome than walking into a party and wondering if you've come to the right place because you don't recognise ANYONE. If this is the case, don't panic and scuttle away — think of all those hours spent knocking together your impressive appearance! Let yourself get used to the near darkness and deafening music and you'll soon begin to relax. Grabbing a Coke should help you to feel less lost, too. Have a walk round and if you still can't see anybody you know, not even the person giving the party, start to look for people who appear to be in the same position as you. Go over and have a chat with them, then you'll be putting both of you at ease!

If no-one comes to ask you to dance straight away, don't just stand at the side of the room looking miserable. Join in by yourself or with a friend; no-one notices who's dancing with who, anyway! Just enjoy the atmosphere — you don't need a boy to get a buzz out of it.

Once you've been to a few parties, you'll wonder what you made all the fuss about the first time! ●

FIRST JOB

IF you're starting a job on a full-time basis or are on a Youth Training Scheme, it will open up a whole new world to you and maybe seem like a terrifying prospect. So much of our lives are spent at school, we get used to the routine and security it provides. Every day we face the same teachers, the same friends, and the same sort of work. Then, suddenly, as well as bringing independence, you'll find that a new job could also mean deadlines, managerial pressure and stress.

Learning your job could take hours or months, depending upon the type of employment. When you start, you may not be given training and will be expected to just pick it up as you go along.

Trying to follow what everyone else does may seem difficult to you at first but you will learn. If you don't understand something, ASK. Even if it has been explained to you more than once and you still don't understand, ask somebody else or ask them to go through it with you, if possible. It's better to do this than make a pig's ear of it! By the 13th week of your new job you will probably have received your written contract, which should be kept in a safe place.

Give yourself a fair chance to find out every aspect of the job, before you decide you don't like it — don't give in your notice at the end of your first day!

One of the best parts of any job, of course, is receiving a juicy paypacket regularly and the first time this happens you'll probably be under the illusion you're rolling in it! Before you start splurging madly, make a list of what needs paying for. Now you're working, you'll have to support yourself to some extent.

Perhaps you have accommodation to pay for, or a contribution towards your keep if you're staying at home, as well as lunches and travel. Whether you get paid weekly or monthly, learn from the start to budget yourself properly.

Very often a first job isn't all we'd like it to be. Everyone has to start somewhere and this is usually at the bottom. All through your working life, you'll be gaining valuable experience which will be useful in your future career. Those people you're running around and making coffee for now, probably had to do the same when they started out! ●

THE Waiting Game

Sarah knew what it was to be kept waiting by people. But when she didn't even know who it was she was waiting for, she wondered if it was really worth it . . .

S ARAH looked at her watch for perhaps the seventh time that evening.

"They're late," she muttered.

"Not by mine, they're not," Rachel said, wiggling her wrist in front of Sarah's nose. "Two minutes to go."

"OK. Two minutes. I'll wait another two minutes and that's all," Sarah said. "Sitting on the wall outside the pictures brings it all back to me, Rachel. I think maybe I'm going to be sick."

"Hey," Rachel said, putting her arm round Sarah's shoulders. "Tony's not like Craig."

"You promised me you'd never say his name again. Now I really am going to be sick!" Sarah howled.

"Look, I know you went through a bad time with you-know-who. I know he stood you up — and two-timed you. I know he stood you up so many times, and even when he did turn up, he wasn't worth waiting for, but we've been through all this over and over again. He was a pig, and you put up with it for too long, and now you're blaming yourself for being too soft. But all boys aren't like him, Sarah. Take this Tony, for instance . . ."

"No thanks."

"What do you mean, 'no thanks'! Look, they'll be here in a minute, and you promised me . . ."

"One minute. That's all. Who is this Tony, anyway?" Sarah groaned.

Tony stopped dead in his tracks, just as he and Paul were about to turn the corner.

"I've changed my mind," he said.

"You what?" Paul spluttered.

"Sorry, Paul. I just can't go through with it," he said. "I must've been mad to let you talk me into it. I'm going home."

"Here! Hang on!" Paul yelled, grabbing him by the collar as he made to rush off. "The girls'll be waiting for us. Do us a favour, Tony? Just this once."

"You've got to be joking!"

"No way," Tony said, defiantly.

"It's a favour," Paul begged. "Look, this afternoon, I explained it all, and you said you would go through with it, didn't you? She's a nice girl, Sarah. But she went out with this boy who messed her around so much that she's got a bit of a complex about

it." Tony looked quite unimpressed.

"So now Rachel's spending all her free time round at Sarah's, and then, when I do get a chance to see her, she keeps on about what happened to her mate, and all that. We thought it'd be a good idea for Sarah to meet someone normal . . ."

"Like me? You've got to be joking!" Tony laughed.

"You've seen what happens to me whenever I get near a female. My mouth won't open. Or, if it does, glugging sounds are all that come out. I'm not the right person for this job. Find someone else. Please."

"Come on, Tony. She's not bad-looking. In fact, she's quite pretty if you like the tearful type . . ."

"Oh no! I can't cope with tears as well." Tony

felt totally out of his depth. "I can't go through with it. I just can't!"

"You've got to. Someone's got to get her over Craig Maitland," Paul said tugging at his elbow. Tony's expression hardened.

"Craig Maitland? The poser from the judo club? Him with the designer hair-cut and the beat-up Escort? Him?" Tony breathed. "She went out with that idiot?"

"Her, and a thousand others,

A short story by Barbara Jacobs.

him, eh? You're going to have to take a chance eventually."

"He's tall, dark and handsome. And very nervous. Scared stiff of girls, apparently. I've never met him, but Paul says he's OK. That means he's great."

"H'mmm." Sarah furrowed her eyebrows. "I think I'll find out some other time. Listen, Rachel, I'm sorry about this. I know you've done your best for me, but I don't want to get paired off with someone you've never even met, do I? I mean, what if we don't hit it off?

"I can't see anything"

"Sshh," Rachel whispered. "He's here."

Sarah turned to look in the direction Rachel was smiling in.

"Where?"

"Over there, with Paul," Rachel hissed. "Just coming round the corner."

"I can't see anything," Sarah muttered.

"Haven't you got your contact lenses in?" Rachel snapped.

Sarah shook her head. "They get all fuzzed up when I cry and I thought I might cry in the pictures and . . ."

"There she is!" Paul murmured. "What d'you think?"

"Which one of the two blobs is she? The pink blob or the green blob?" Tony asked.

"The pink one. Where's your glasses?"

"Couldn't wear them on a date, could I?" Tony muttered.

"How're you going to see the film?" Paul sighed.

"With difficulty," Tony admitted.

Paul put his hand on Tony's shoulder as they reached the girls, ready

for introduction . . .

"Drongo!" Sarah shouted, delightedly. "Hey, Drongo, it really is you, isn't it?"

Rachel stared at her in disbelief. Paul's eyebrows arched questioningly at Rachel.

"Ratsy?" Tony laughed. "Hey, Ratsy! Haven't seen you for years and years."

"Not since Infants' School." Sarah laughed, jumping up and throwing her arms round him.

"Hey, you've grown up to be really pretty!" Tony laughed, joining her on the wall again.

"You're not too bad yourself!" Sarah grinned, ruffling his hair.

"Remember when I used to untie your pony-tail in reading lessons?"

"Remember kiss-chase?"

"Remember Miss Lorrimer? Fat Miss Lorrimer?" Tony asked.

"Sarah, this is Tony. Tony, this is Sarah," Rachel said, looking at Paul with a huge smile on her face.

But neither of them were listening. Arm in arm, deep in conversation and laughter, they were walking away.

"Fancy a burger? Catch up with old times?" Tony was saying.

"Great! What about those two, though?" Sarah asked.

"They can go to the pictures, can't they, just the two of them? Now, how come you moved out to the new estate . . . ?"

Rachel and Paul watched them go, staring after them as if they were two aliens, Drongo and Ratsy, suddenly on their home planet.

"I told you it would work out," Rachel said.

"Never doubted it for a minute," Paul smiled. □

probably," Paul agreed.

"I can't stand him," Tony snarled. "He needs treading on."

"Well, what're we waiting for?" Paul grinned.

"I don't think going out with his ex is a way of treading on him," Tony said, doubtfully.

"It's the best way," Paul said. "Let's go."

"It's a minute past," Sarah announced. "That's it. Time's up. I'm definitely off."

"Where to?" Rachel asked.

"Home, of course.

I've wasted enough evenings at this wall. It's about time I did something else."

"So, what're you going to do when you get home? Wash your hair? Howl over all your old records? Face it, Sarah, you're going to miss the chance of a lifetime."

"What chance of a lifetime?" Sarah sneered.

"Tony. He'll be here in a minute. Sure to be, because Paul's with him, and Paul's never more than minute or two late. Just wait to see

A FRIEND INDEED!

For a shoulder to cry on, for someone to listen to you moaning daily about the size of your nose, for help on how to attract that gorgeous hunk and, of course, for the occasional argument, your best friend will always be there for you. "Jackie" asks some of you lot what keeps you and your bestest chum together through thick and thin . . .

KATIE and MICHELLE, both 16, met at school five years ago and immediately hit it off. Their similar sense of humour helped make the rest of school time "a great laugh". Since then they really have been inseparable — even choosing the same options so they could stay together!

Katie and Michelle enjoy jaunting off with each other to parties, for meals and shopping sprees. Katie says, "I value her judgment on clothes."

Before parties, the girls often experiment with make-up and new hair-styles on each other although Katie admits, "I wouldn't collect the milk off the doorstep after Michelle has done me up, never mind go to a party!

"We go to concerts too. The last one we went to was T'Pau but we'd love to go to a Deacon Blue concert, or an INXS concert, a Heart concert, a . . ." OK, girls, save this for begging outside the booking office!

"Most of the time, though, we talk — on the 'phone, at school and at each other's houses. Well, at least we used to talk on the phone a lot but Mum wasn't too pleased with the last phone-bill. I suppose we'll just have to tie two empty yoghurt cartons on the ends of a piece of string from now on!"

Katie says, "I can trust her not to tell anybody the personal things I confide in her." Michelle adds, "This friendship is so valuable, we can always sort things out and get a good perspective on a situation."

No problems are too difficult for the girls to solve. When Katie was going out with her boyfriend, they formed a foursome so they could still be together. Katie assures her friend, "Our friendship is more important than boyfriends . . ." but with after-thought she continues ". . . unless of course I was going out with Tom Cruise."

Michelle interrupts. "We have had some awful experiences together though. Once we were walking down the street and some workmen whistled at us. Katie says she was trying to walk faster to get away but, really, I think she was putting too much energy into trying to wiggle her bum, but anyway," (just as the story begins to resemble one of Ronnie Corbet's v. long-winded jokes), she continues, "she slipped and her shoe went flying into the air!"

Er, yes, maybe it was one of those incidents that you had to be there to appreciate!

AIDAN (18) and CAROL (17) have been best friends since they first played together as a pair of cutie five-year-olds! Although different sexes, they find this is an advantage as they can learn about what it's like being a boy/girl — which helps them with other relationships. They live very near each other so they get together quite a lot, especially, Aidan says, when Carol is in a bad mood and needs someone to shout and scream at! Carol has even been known to cross the road to see Aidan at 3 a.m. but criticises Aidan for not being that interested in her problems at that time in the morning! But, of course, like any friendship, it works both ways as Aidan, thankfully, isn't the stereotyped, macho type who never admits to having problems. Aidan says, "I can tell her all my innermost thoughts and not be embarrassed."

Of course, they have their fall-outs just like everybody else and, once at school, they had a real girlie-girlie fight, (Aidan shamefacedly remembers), by pulling each other's hair etc., until Aidan decided to give in as Carol had the unfair advantage of a pair of high-heeled shoes! Just like most 'heated discussions' that seem extremely important at the time, they can't even remember what it was about.

Aidan likes Carol's honesty. "She never breaks a promise. In fact, once she said she'd throw a very hot cup of coffee all over me if I didn't stop annoying her. Unfortunately she kept her promise that time, too!"

DAMIAN and MARCUS (both 15) got together at school in first year after a school exam. Damian noticed Marcus in the huge hall writing non-stop for the three-hour exam, while he was just sitting transfixed with his blank page. Damian was so impressed he thought Marcus would be a worthwhile mate, so he introduced himself after the ordeal.

After a while they realised they had a lot in common. They both liked Bros, Brother Beyond, U2 and Michael Jackson. Damian is a bit of a manager for Marcus' group, "Richer Dust", since he isn't exactly musically talented himself. Having said this, he *can* play a couple of ditties on his flute, but, strangely enough, can't seem to find a market for this in the pop world! He's quick, however, to do his Arthur Daley impression — "My talents lie elsewhere, I can assure you, my son!"

Neither of the boys will admit to pouring out their troubles to the other — "We don't usually talk about girls, it's not the thing to do." Well, us girlies must be either much too uninteresting a subject or the boys are scared to lose their mucho macho image! "We prefer to go out together to wild parties, concerts and the cinema, than just sitting moaning to each other." For boys who never talk about girls though, Damian goes on to say that Marcus sometimes fixes him up with a girl he doesn't want to go out with. And they're still friends? "Oh, yeah, but we fall out quite a lot — it would get boring otherwise!"

TONIA and ANDREA (both 16) met each other thirteen years ago at a really swish theatrical event — a pantomime performance of Mother Goose! Tonia and Andrea grew up to be the type that stay at each other's houses just to talk the socks off one another. "At 2 a.m., I'll be bleary-eyed and Andrea will be saying, 'But, Tonia, what do you think I should do about . . .'" Tonia says. "Sometimes we do go out together, usually in a group, but it depends on mood and money."

On the subject of boyfriends, they both say that they'd never give up their friendship, "which comes first", and they would somehow manage to make time for both. In fact, like true friends, they help each other get the man of their dreams but usually not in the way the other would have planned it. Such plans as telling a boy that their friend fancies him and hoping he gets the hint, is not unknown! Also, Tonia once invited Andrea round to her house to find, surprise surprise, the boy that she'd only yesterday told Tonia she fancied. "Subtlety is definitely not Tonia's strong point!" reckons Andrea.

"We enjoy a great giggle together, although I must amdit it's usually me laughing at Tonia, she can be so silly; like the time when she burnt her feet and couldn't wear shoes. She wasn't going to miss the disco though, so she went in her pink furry slippers instead!"

Hope that comment doesn't cause Tonia to go in a huff — last time they tiffed, it took a whopping whole school term for them to make up again! "Jackie" exits quickly, just in case!

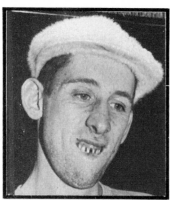

Shane McGowan (The Pogues) . . . to visit the dentist!

Colin Vearncombe . . . to keep looking for the next Black hit!

Morten Harket . . . to remember to get dressed before the gig!

Sam Brown . . . to find out where that button went!

RESO

New Year's resolutions are the easiest thing in the world to make . . . and break! If you can even *remember* what your resolutions were last year, then you're streets ahead of everyone in this office.

However, we *have* been able to compile a list of resolutions that we think the rich 'n' famous should be making this year. Somehow, we don't think they will but, if they did, we wonder how long they'd keep them.

Debbie Harry . . . to try waxing my arms!

George Michael . . . to invest in a new Gilette!

Captain (Canute) Sensible . . . that the tide shall not come in!

Wendy James (Transvision Vamp) . . . to try a new shade of lipstick!

Luke Goss . . . to buy a new pair of jeans!

I've . . .

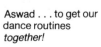

Aswad . . . to get our dance routines *together!*

IS IT THE REAL THING...
(OR JUST A CRUSH)?

He may be someone you already know or a hunk you've admired from afar, but, either way, just seeing him sets your heart a-flutter. But how can you be sure it's love and not just a l-u-u-rve attack? Our foolproof posers will reveal whether or not your feelings for him are the real thing . . .

1. When you first caught sight of him, did you . . .
c. think he was nice, but decide it takes more than good looks for you to fall for someone,
b. fall instantly in love but spend a lot of time pretending not to notice him, or,
a. have to reinsert your eyeballs after they popped out of your head at the sheer gorgeousness of him?

2. When you first spoke to him, was it . . .
b. what? You haven't spoken to him yet, or,
a. great! You got to examine his handsome jawline up close, or,
c. great! You couldn't wait to speak to him again?

3. Suppose you were in a supermarket when you noticed him standing by the fresh vegetables. Would you . . .
a. "accidentally" bump into him, allowing you to grab hold of his muscular arm for support,
c. walk up to him and say hello and get into a conversation about salads, or,
b. study him from behind the baked beans till he leaves?

4. The last time you saw him you . . .
a. went red, pulled your earlobes nervously and kicked yourself later for your lack of control,
c. spent your time trying to catch his eye to see if he's got the same gooey look you have, or,
b. can't remember what you did, it was all so wonderful?

5. The man of your dreams is away for the weekend when you see a completely gorgeous hunk in the street. What do you think?
c. "Hmm, maybe if I had a guy like that on my arm then John (or whoever) would notice me."
a. "Mmm, yes, he's a bit of all right".
b. Nothing. You were so busy daydreaming about THE man that you didn't notice.

6. You hear that he's going to see a particularly long and arty French film at a snoot cinema. Would you . . .
b. buy a magazine about new-wave French cinema,
a. stay in and do your nails — nothing is worth two hours of subtitles, or,
c. get dressed up and go yourself in the hope that you can meet him and pretend you always go to those sort of films?

7. You meet his best friend in a record shop. Do you see this as . . .
b. an opportunity to stammer and look nervous again, making sure you talk about everything but HIM,
a. the perfect time to drop a few hints about how much you fancy lover boy, or,
c. a chance to find out what kind of music he likes?

8. You see him sitting with a pretty girl in the Wimpy Bar. She is obviously . . .
a. some floozy he's picked up. Ah well, you'll no doubt get over him soon enough,
b. another girl who worships the ground he walks upon. You can't blame him for being so wonderful, or,
c. his sister, or just a friend, or something. You're sure it couldn't be a girlfriend.

9. You and some friends meet him and his pals at a party and you all get talking. How does he behave in your company?
c. He sends the odd glance in your direction.
a. He touches your arm occasionally as you're talking.
b. He gives you the same amount of attention as everyone else.

10. You see him one day wearing the most awfully naff clothes. Do you . . .
b. not notice — there's nothing he could wear that he wouldn't look great in,
c. put it down to the fact that most boys have no sense of style and given half the chance you could straighten him out, or,
a. think it's a bit embarrassing, but at least it shows he has a sense of humour?

11. Suppose you spotted him out shopping with his mother, and he sees you too. How do you think he would react? Would he . . .
c. bring his mum over for a chat,
b. give you a quick wave before going back to what he was doing, or,
a. say hello, though it's obvious he's a little embarrassed?

12. You hear that he likes a girl with a sense of humour. Do you . . .
a. memorise a few one-liners from a comedy show and hope he hasn't seen it,
c. make sure your laugh-a-minute friend isn't around whenever you see him, or,
b. laugh loudly at practically everything he says?

13. A friend of his is showing you some pictures he took recently. The man of your dreams appears in one. Do you . . .
a. stare in awe at how well he photographs,
c. ask if you can have a copy 6" x 8" and one wallet-sized, or,
b. try not to make it too obvious how that particular photo holds your attention?

14. Supposing he phones you up to ask if you're coming to a concert he and some friends are going to. Would you be . . .
b. terrified. Suppose you muck it up and the night's a disaster,
a. too busy planning your outfit to worry about anything else, or,
c. ecstatic, but worried about whether or not it means anything?

15. At a disco, you finally decide you've got to make the big move. Do you . . .
b. chicken out, realising that he's bound to turn you down,
a. wrap your arms round him and give him a major smackeroonie, or,
c. tell him how you feel, and hope desperately that he feels the same way for you?

Mostly A's
This isn't love — just a healthy case of attraction, that's all! Of course, the real thing may not be very far away, but for the moment, you may be quite content to keep things on a "you fancy him — he fancies you" basis. And if the occasional snog is enough to sustain your interest in him, that's fine. But, remember, you may not feel quite so strongly about going shopping for new shoes with him. That being the case, be very careful when it comes to whispering sweet nothings in his ear — allowing him to believe that you're more slushy about him than you actually are can be a major mistake.

Mostly B's
This is a bit dodgy this one. Not only are you suffering from a crush of major proportions, but it seems like the bloke in question is just not interested. Your feelings for this person may seem very strong, but it's likely that you just don't know him well enough for these feelings to be justified. This lack of communication may have led you to build him up into an almost perfect person, but, of course, this is hardly likely to be the case in reality. Maybe if you conquered your sense of wonder enough to approach him, you might be able to start a more realistic relationship. Be careful, though, for there's a big possibility of disillusionment.

Mostly C's
Yup, no doubt about it, this is the big one — you're in love! Your feelings for this person are not confined to the way they look or how well they kiss. You love them for who they are and are well aware of their faults, but accept even their nasty habit of nail-biting and their short temper because this is "lurvesville". If you haven't told the lucky man of your feelings towards him then do so right away, that way you can get on with all those important lovey-dovey activities like holding hands and staring for hours on end into each other's eyes.

SAY HELLO, WAVE GOODBYE

"MY FAMILY HAD MOVED TO CAMFIELD NEARLY SIX MONTHS AGO, BUT I STILL HADN'T SETTLED DOWN . . ."

"MY MIND WAS STILL BACK IN WAYBRIDGE WITH IAN, MY BOYFRIEND . . ."

"ONE MORNING . . ."

HAPPY BIRTHDAY, LISA. THE POST'S JUST ARRIVED. HERE'S THE BIGGEST ONE — IT'S GOT A WAYBRIDGE POSTMARK . . .

OH, GREAT. THANKS, MUM. IT'S IAN'S WRITING — I KNEW HE WOULDN'T FORGET . . .

LOOK, MUM, ISN'T IT LOVELY . . . ?

AND I WAS GETTING WORRIED BECAUSE HIS LETTERS WERE GETTING SHORTER AND SHORTER. BUT THIS CARD PROVES HE MUST STILL LOVE ME AS MUCH AS EVER . . .

OH, A NEW WATCH! IT'S LOVELY! THANKS, MUM . . .

AND THERE'S ANOTHER PRESENT TO COME. WE'RE GOING BACK TO WAYBRIDGE FOR THE DAY ON SATURDAY, TO SEE AUNT HELEN AND UNCLE MIKE . . .

"AND THAT WAS THE PRESENT THAT REALLY MADE MY DAY . . ."

"ALL DAY AT SCHOOL, I WAS BUBBLING OVER WITH EXCITEMENT . . ."

HAPPY BIRTHDAY, LISA. HEY, HOW ABOUT COMING TO THE DISCO ON FRIDAY TO CELEBRATE?

THANKS, PAUL, BUT I'M HAVING AN EARLY NIGHT ON FRIDAY. I'VE TO BE UP EARLY ON SATURDAY MORNING — I'M GOING BACK TO WAYBRIDGE FOR THE DAY.

PAUL'S REALLY NICE, BUT THERE'S NO POINT IN ENCOURAGING HIM. NOT WHEN I'LL BE SEEING IAN AGAIN ON SATURDAY. IT'LL BE LIKE I'VE NEVER BEEN AWAY — ALL THE PEOPLE AND PLACES I LOVE . . .

"EARLY ON SATURDAY MORNING . . ."

YOU LOOK HAPPIER TODAY THAN YOU HAVE IN MONTHS, LISA.

I AM, MUM. OH, I KNOW WE HAD TO MOVE BECAUSE OF DAD'S JOB, AND CAMFIELD'S ALL RIGHT, I SUPPOSE, BUT IT'S NOT LIKE HOME . . .

"AND, LATER . . ."

AUNT HELEN, UNCLE MIKE! YOU HAVEN'T CHANGED A BIT!

YOU HAVE, THOUGH, LISA. YOU LOOK A COUPLE OF INCHES TALLER THAN WHEN YOU MOVED AWAY!

I KNOW YOU'RE DYING TO HAVE A LOOK ROUND THE OLD PLACE, LISA, SO WHY DON'T YOU GO FOR A WALK WHILE WE'RE GETTING LUNCH READY?

WELL, IF YOU'RE SURE YOU DON'T MIND. MAYBE I'LL SEE SOME OF MY OLD FRIENDS FROM SCHOOL . . .

"I DID. THERE, JUST GOING INTO OLD MRS WALTON'S SWEET SHOP, WAS SARAH . . ."

HEY, IT ISN'T A SWEET SHOP ANY MORE!

LISA! WHAT ARE YOU DOING HERE?

MUM AND DAD BROUGHT ME BACK FOR THE DAY TO SEE MY AUNT AND UNCLE. BUT WHAT'S HAPPENED TO OLD MRS WALTON AND HER SUGAR MICE?

OF COURSE, YOU WON'T KNOW. SHE SOLD UP TWO MONTHS AGO. SHE'S GONE UP NORTH TO LIVE WITH HER DAUGHTER.

HOW'S SUSAN? SHE HASN'T WRITTEN TO ME IN WEEKS.

SUSAN? OH, ER . . . SHE'S ALL RIGHT. I — I'VE GOT TO DASH. SEE YOU!

I WONDER WHAT'S WRONG WITH SARAH? IT ISN'T LIKE HER TO BE SO OFF-HAND . . .

"BUT I WAS ON MY WAY TO SEE IAN, AND THAT WAS ALL THAT MATTERED . . ."

I'M GLAD I DIDN'T LET IAN KNOW I WAS COMING. I'LL BET HE GETS A REAL SURPRISE WHEN HE SEES ME . . .

"HE CERTAINLY DID . . ."

LISA!

WE DIDN'T EXPECT TO SEE YOU BACK HERE . . .

OBVIOUSLY NOT!

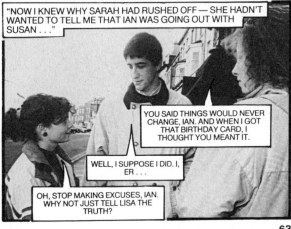

"NOW I KNEW WHY SARAH HAD RUSHED OFF — SHE HADN'T WANTED TO TELL ME THAT IAN WAS GOING OUT WITH SUSAN . . ."

YOU SAID THINGS WOULD NEVER CHANGE, IAN. AND WHEN I GOT THAT BIRTHDAY CARD, I THOUGHT YOU MEANT IT.

WELL, I SUPPOSE I DID. I, ER . . .

OH, STOP MAKING EXCUSES, IAN. WHY NOT JUST TELL LISA THE TRUTH?

LISA, I'M SORRY. BUT YOU'RE SO FAR AWAY NOW, AND SUSAN AND I — WELL, WE'VE ALWAYS BEEN FRIENDLY. BUT I DID FEEL GUILTY, AND THAT'S WHY I SENT THE CARD.

WE SHOULD HAVE WRITTEN AND TOLD YOU, LISA. I'M SORRY, TOO.

SO AM I — FOR BEING STUPID ENOUGH TO BELIEVE THINGS WOULD STAY THE SAME. I — I'D BETTER GO BACK TO AUNT HELEN'S, I SUPPOSE. THEY'LL BE WONDERING WHERE I'VE GOT TO . . .

SEE YOU, LISA . . .

"BUT I WALKED BACK SLOWLY, TO GIVE MYSELF TIME TO THINK . . ."

THIS PLACE IS JUST THE WAY I REMEMBER IT. IT'S US — IAN AND SUSAN AND ME — WHO'VE CHANGED. AND I'M THE ONE WHO DOESN'T BELONG HERE ANY MORE . . .

"SO . . ."

YOU DON'T LOOK TOO HAPPY, LISA. DIDN'T YOU FIND ANY OF YOUR OLD FRIENDS?

OH, YES. I SAW THEM ALL. BUT SOMEHOW THERE WASN'T VERY MUCH TO SAY ANY MORE . . .

"THAT EVENING . . ."

GOODBYE, AND COME BACK SOON, EH?

WE WILL, AND THANKS FOR A LOVELY DAY.

BUT I'M NOT IN ANY HURRY TO COME BACK HERE ANY MORE . . .

"NEXT DAY I WENT FOR A LONG WALK BY MYSELF AROUND CAMFIELD . . ."

IT'S FUNNY, BUT I NEVER NOTICED HOW NICE THAT OLD CHURCH WAS BEFORE. AND THAT PARK . . . MAYBE CAMFIELD ISN'T SUCH A BAD PLACE AFTER ALL. ONLY I WAS SO BUSY DREAMING OF WAYBRIDGE AND IAN, I KEPT MY EYES SHUT . . .

"NEXT MORNING . . ."

HI, LISA. DID YOU ENJOY YOUR TRIP BACK HOME?

TO WAYBRIDGE? YOU KNOW, I'VE JUST REALISED SOMETHING, PAUL. CAMFIELD IS MY HOME NOW. I CAN'T GO ON LOOKING BACK FOR EVER, CAN I?

SOME OF US ARE GOING TO THE PICTURES TOMORROW NIGHT. DO YOU FANCY COMING, LISA?

THANKS, PAUL. I'D REALLY LIKE THAT . . .

PART OF ME STILL FEELS SAD ABOUT IAN. BUT THAT'S OVER NOW. AND I'M READY FOR NEW FRIENDS — ESPECIALLY PAUL!

"I'D COME HOME, AT LAST . . ."

THE END

A TOUCH OF CLASS

SOME THINGS NEVER GO OUT OF STYLE — LIKE THIS CLASSY COLLECTION NO WARDROBE SHOULD BE WITHOUT . . .

BLÅCK MAGIC

Inside every stylish wardrobe is a little black dress. Go for the cling if you're skinny or straighter silhouettes if you're more well-endowed! And don't forget to drip diamante for classy nights on the town.

PUTTING ON THE BITS!

Stylish gals know that little things mean a lot. So pile on the style with classic finishing touches — pearls, a Timex watch, floaty silk scarves, a boxy handbag and black stockings. Beauty-wise, go for scarlet lips, a pale complexion and a snoot scent like Chanel No. 5.

SUIT YOURSELF!

A plain suit is something you can wear just about anywhere. Dress it up with a slinky blouse, lots of jewellery and high heels or, for a more casual look, choose a cotton shirt, opaque tights and flat shoes.

TAKING THE ROUGH WITH THE SMOOTH

Blue denim never goes out of style. Tough jeans and jackets mix well with a bit of chic — a silk scarf. Suede college loafers and belts come high on the classic list, too!

GOOD FOUNDATIONS

It's no good wearing super-swish clothes if what's underneath is a shambles! Invest in some silky undies for undercover glamour. Pretty teddies, body stockings, high-cut briefs and camisole sets will make sure you feel great from the inside out!

KNIT-WITS

Chunky Arans and lacy cardigans are hard to beat for snuggly style! Choose classy colours such as ivory, peach and taupe and quality yarns like lambswool, angora or Shetland. They'll last loads longer than cheapie acrylic!

PEOPLE OF AUSTRALIA

Dame Edna Everage — *the best legs this side of an emu?*

The Housewife:

Dame Edna Everage, housewife and superstar, enjoys nothing more than preparing meals for her circle of friends, which includes such successful people as Dallas oil-magnate, J.R. Ewing. If she wears the same dress twice, it's only because there's a dressmakers' strike on.

The Policeman:

Mad Max is a fine example of the Australian traffic cop who doesn't think that just because there's been a nuclear war, motorists have a right to ignore the Highway Code. Drive carefully now, Max!

The Career Woman:

Charlene Mitchell began her working career as an apprentice mechanic but, not long before her marriage to Scott Robinson, changed her name to Kylie Minogue and found fame and fortune as a pop star.

The Family Pet:

Rather than settle for a cat or a dog, the average Australian household would rather choose a kangaroo for a pet. The 'roos are given names like Skippy and, in some cases, become television stars in their own right. Alternatively, they can be trained and entered for boxing matches. Kangaroos like to eat crops and damage fences.

The Politician:

Sir Leslie Patterson, Minister for Culture, Wine and Cheese, is a bit of a bon viveur and, when he's miles away from home and his good wife, Lady Gwen, he likes nothing more than partaking of a drop of a good vintage in pleasant company. However, Les's 'friends' are less likely to be found on the business pages of the morning's newspapers than on Page Three.

Sir Les Patterson — *the more mature woman's hunk of Australian beefcake!*

THE LOW-DOWN ON DOWN-UNDER

● Australia has become more and more familiar to us over the past few years, helped by the number of Aussie soaps on British TV and the number of bands and personalities who became stars during the 80's.

So, stuff your head into a hat with corks on, spread some Vegemite on your Mighty White and shift your laughing tackle in to top gear before delving into our mini-Encyclopaedia Australis(!).

AUSTRALIAN HISTORY — THE ALTERNATIVE VERSION!

Australia is probably the world's most amazing continent, simply because no-one can come up with a reasonable explanation for the number of evolutionary disasters which it has produced.

Take the kangaroo, for instance. This animal could be adequately described as a cross between a mouse and a Scotsman — complete with built-in sporran!

The Platypus — *was it an accident?*

Even more astounding is the platypus, a furry duck with four legs which swims underwater and lays eggs. Whoever thought that one up must've been completely off their trolley!

It fitted in quite well, though, with the koala, which can only eat the leaves of the eucalyptus tree, and the emu, a cross between the chicken and the giraffe.

These animals, although completely ridiculous, are relatively harmless, but the same can't be said for the native reptiles and insects. Australia has the dubious honour of being home to more varieties of poisonous beastie than the rest of the world put together.

One of the most worrying creepy-crawlies is a little spider that sits underneath the toilet seat and jumps out and bites you when you're at your most vulnerable. Fortunately, the poison is rarely fatal, although the shock often comes close!

Anyway, once the animals had settled down in Oz, Mr & Mrs Homo Sapiens arrived. Back in the early days, the Aborigines were a curious bunch of folk who thought that a hollow tree was something called a 'didgeridoo' and was for blowing through and creating music. How wrong they were! All the 'didgeridoo' managed to produce was a low monotonous tone which was in no way complemented by their other musical instrument, the wobble board.

It was in their search for a new way of making music that they discovered their only major contribution to the western world — the coat-hanger! Unfortunately, since he didn't wear clothes and had no use for a coat-hanger, the inventor threw it away and the patent was finally given to an enterprising Westerner a few centuries later.

The original inventor did have some reward for his labours, however, when the chunk of wood he'd flung away in frustration made a U-turn, flew back and knocked his wife unconscious. This, he realised, was a very useful implement. He called it a 'boomerang', from the old Aborigine word meaning 'wife silencer', and was soon the toast of the tribe. (Er, are you quite sure about this? — Ed.)

Talking of tribes, the Aborigines had some rather peculiar practices which decided whether or not an individual could become a member of the gang.

They not only requested that the poor unfortunate should jump out of a tall tree and drink blood, but also that he have his front two teeth knocked out, without anaesthetic, to prove his manhood.

Anyway, a few hundred years later, Captain Cook discovered Australia and claimed it for the British Empire. Needless to say, the natives were slightly unchuffed at this and even more so when the Brits decided to turn their beloved Australia into a gigantic prison, and transport all their criminals there.

Even the criminal element in Blighty weren't too keen on the idea and many of them begged to be executed rather than spend the rest of their lives half-way

Two kangaroos — or is it Kylie and Jason on a Stock, Aitken and Waterman video shoot?

around the globe. This was the general opinion of most of the British public until Captain Cook's son, Thomas, set up the world's first travel agent's, explained to everyone the benefits of living in Australia, and, as a special offer, gave discounts to TV producers and anyone named Bruce or Sheila. It was an enormous success.

Soon, people had emigrated to this wonderful new land and discovered that, as the only habitable area was the coastline, they had to build their houses facing the ocean. This meant that

Mel Gibson in "Mad Max" — a hunk of Australian beefcake.

everyone had a back garden that extended for hundreds of miles into the heart of the continent. This became known as "the bit out the back" which, in turn, was shortened to "the outback".

This arid no-man's-land was eventually handed over to the Aborigines, whom it belonged to anyway, so that the settlers could fairly lay claim to all the lovely bits of luscious, green coastline. Thus Australia was 'born'!

Although now an independently governed colony, the Australians just can't leave us alone and seem determined to turn us all mad. This they have done by saturation coverage of Australian life through a host of soap operas, comedies and documentaries.

The leader of this cultural attack is none other than Rolf Harris, who crept up on an unsuspecting public some years back with such innocuous-sounding ditties as "Two Little Boys" and "Tie Me Kangaroo Down, Sport" but who was soon encouraging vandalism and grafitti by painting pictures and slogans on walls, live on television. As if this wasn't enough, he began to indoctrinate British children, as presenter of "Cartoon Time" and even had the majority of under-11's believing that the didgeridoo was a valid musical instrument.

Is it any wonder, then, that when these children grew up they were prepared for "Neighbours", "Prisoner: Cell Block H" and "Richmond Hill"?

QUALITY TELEVISION (?)

Neighbours
All about the daily life of the inhabitants of Ramsay Street. Lots of families who seem to have no social life beyond the end of the street and spend just as much time in each others' houses as they do in their own.

The Sullivans
Almost a period drama, set in the 40's. Possibly the most patriotic family in Australia, the Sullivans have been fighting the Second World War for over ten years.

Young Doctors
Doctors and nurses fall in and out of love in a small hospital. In the early days of the series, the budget was so low that they didn't have any scenery and all the action happened in front of a row of hospital curtain screens.

Flying Doctors
Same as above, but these doctors are in the heart of the outback and have aeroplanes instead of ambulances. Everyone they treat seems to be at death's door but miraculously recovers.

Prisoner: Cell Block H
Just another soap opera but set in a women's prison. In Australia it's known simply as Prisoner, but British TV bosses thought the public might confuse it with the old Patrick McGoohan series. Fat chance! Who *is* Number One, anyway?

SOME AUSTRALIAN MOVIES

(P.S. Australia is not famous for its movie industry. Wonder why?)

The Cars That Ate Paris (1974)
Not Paris, France, and not Paris, Texas, but Paris, Australia! Paris is a small town in the heart of Australia where cars crash, drivers and passengers end up in hospital, and the cars become the property of the car-crazed townsfolk. Quite mad!

Picnic At Hanging Rock (1975)
A bunch of young ladies go for a picnic in the countryside but three of them disappear in mysterious circumstances. Based on a true story and set at the turn of the century.

The Money Movers (1979)
Adventure and thrills in this tale about a security van that gets robbed. . . erm, that's it!

The Club (1980)
Laughs and drama in the day to day lives of Australian Rules Football players, the only rules of which are "no weapons or motorised transport"!

Mad Max (1981)
Max is an Interceptor, a cop that stops motorists foolish enough to violate the motor laws. The fact that Australia has just been zapped with a goodly dose of radiation and Max is slightly berserk just adds to the fun.

Razorback (1984)
Sheer terror as people left, right and centre fall prey to a ravenous, man-eating pig! Unfortunately for its victims, this little piggy is quite able to huff and puff and blow their houses down. Alternatively, it just rushes headlong through the wall! I mean, would you believe an old man who claims his grandchild has just been stolen by 900 lb of bacon?

DO NOT DIS

GARY

"The cine camera I'm holding is wonderful! I've always been interested in film-making and even though my camera is a bit prehistoric, it's perfect for making home movies with. The only problem is, everyone I know suffers from cinephobia, so if I want to catch them acting naturally I've got to be sneaky about it! OK, so I'm not Alfred Hitchcock but even he had to start somewhere!

"This pile of litter in front of me actually has a use — it's my comics. I bought them all when I was at school (honest!) and although I suppose it's a bit silly keeping them, I'm sentimental that way! They're easy reading if I'm not in the mood for reading a huge book. There's a lot more where these came from, too!

"And as for my plants, well, my plants are my friends — it's nice to have someone to talk to late at night. I'm a bit strange that way!

"The TV is indispensible, I'm afraid. I'm a really lazy person at heart, so if watching a documentary about Polish politics takes up less energy than writing a letter, I'll watch TV every time.

"In my opinion, everyone should have a poster of Spock. He's a great guy. I mean, who else can say, "Scanners indicate an energy of a type never before encountered, Captain," and raise his eyebrows at the same time?

"My book collection has dwindled a bit — I used to have tons of really awful pulp science-fiction novels. Unfortunately, I sold most of them while I was broke! My mum's quite happy about that, though — she said they were rotting my brain."

URB!

J O

"This door is completely covered by my postcard collection. I didn't actually make a conscious decision to start a collection but all my friends seemed to go on holiday and send me interesting cards at once!

"My pinboard is important because it's covered with pictures of people who mean a lot to me and loads of little mementoes from holidays, parties and days out.

"The picture below the pinboard is one my dad made for me. I love it because it's so bright and cheerful and it really makes me feel happy when I've been depressed about something.

"I have a lot of books, because books mean a lot to me — I read constantly. Basically, I'll read anything at all, but my favourite authors are Byron and Asimov (Pretentious, moi?).

"The candle I'm holding is in the shape of a skull. I know it looks pretty creepy but it holds good memories for me. My mum and I were on holiday in Arran a couple of years ago and we went to a great souvenir shop. There I spotted this candle in the window and decided I wasn't leaving the shop until it was mine. I'm very determined at times!

"My little white bear is gorgeous and I love him to bits! Danny (my boyfriend) bought him to cheer me up after I found out I had a £1.50 overdraft. It was a real blow but I got through it — with the bear's help!"

"I won these trophies when I was at primary school. I played tenor horn in a quartet and we won a national competition for brass ensembles. It's the only thing I've ever won and I'm ridiculously proud of it!

"The Hellraiser poster has a special place in my heart as it's my favourite movie of all time. The author and director, Clive Barker, is one of my personal heroes. I don't find his work particularly scary, just incredibly fascinating. I got the poster from my mate, Justin, who's writing a book on British horror films.

"As you can see, I've got rather a lot of books! I tend to buy books compulsively but I *do* read them. They aren't in any particular order and my shelves are pretty untidy but it's easier to borrow books than it is to borrow shelves so, until I return some of the borrowed books or have the time and inclination to build some more shelves, that's how it'll remain!

"The guitar's stored in the corner because I'm not terribly good at playing it. I don't seem to have enough fingers! I know about half a dozen chords, though, and

I can usually find the note I'm looking for if I have a spare ten minutes!

"The boots beside it, I've had for years. I've had to get them repaired a couple of times but they're so comfortable, I couldn't bear to buy a new pair. The ice axe was reduced in a sale a couple of years ago so, in a fit of optimism, I bought it. Needless to say, I've never used it!

"The director's chair is part of my vision of grandeur! I've always wanted to be a movie director but I was turned down for film school when I left college. I'm still determined to do it at some point. Am I eccentric? I hope so!"

DISTURB!

J A Q U I E

"The most valued possessions in my room are my records. My collection varies in size from day to day — I'm always selling off albums, then wishing I hadn't because I'm dying to hear them again! I'd hate to be without music. I love stomping tunes to wake me up in the morning and slushy songs to sit and dream to.

"The stereo is great but cost me about a zillion pounds, so in a way, I wish I'd settled for something second-hand instead! Still, you know what they say about a fool and her money!

"As for the jewellery, well, where would I be without my 'gems'? I feel almost naked unless I have at least one piece of jewellery on and I *always* wear earrings. I love an armful of clanking, jangly bracelets, too. Unusual, second-hand jewellery is always the best and you get that extra sense of achievement when you've rooted through a pile of rubbish to uncover a 'find'!

"To keep all my 'jewels' in, I've got this lovely wooden jewellery box. It was a present from a friend who brought it back from India. It's got a secret way of opening and I love the way it's carved.

"My friend and I were in a little craft shop one day and we saw parasols which I really liked but couldn't afford. She must've remembered, though, because four months later I got this one as part of my Christmas present. It's great for covering up the smashed shade on my lamp and making the room 'dim and interesting'.

"Gavin, the ivy plant, is my most favourite plant ever, though this is probably due to the fact he's the only plant I haven't killed! Pretty surprising, really — considering the number of times I've knocked him over!"

73

HOW THE WEST IS WORN!

Howdy, pardners! Have we rounded up one darn good collection of cowgirl clothes for you! So if you wanna be dressed for the part, saddle yourself with some of these groovy cowgirl goodies!

BOOT-IFUL!

Big black boots finish off the classic cowgirl look (pinch your brother's and wear loads of socks to make them fit!). If all those chains and toe-caps aren't your style, pull on a pair of classic black leather riding boots instead.

CHEEKY!

All that horse-riding's sure hard on your jeans! Cheer up dull denims with a bright scarf and a sheriff's badge to show 'em who's boss!

You'll find a great selection of fun badges in most toy shops.

74

BITS 'N' BOBS

No self-respecting cowgirl would be seen without a smart stetson! Ours is from The Hat Shop, but you'll find hats like it in chain stores everywhere. Add to the Western look with a bootlace tie, pocket handkerchief and cowboy belt.

WHAT A WAIST!

Perfect for chilly nights in the desert, waistcoats give any outfit warmth and style! Choose shades of sand, rust or stone for that authentic 'wagon trail' look!

We found ours in Top Shop, but you could raid jumble sales, charity shops or your grandad's wardrobe!

TRUE BLUE

A classic denim shirt should take pride of place in every cowgirl wardrobe! Ours is by Rocky, but you'll find similar shirts in chain stores everywhere.

BROWNED OFF!

Chase the blues away — swap boring blue denim and get tanned instead! Check out chain stores and specialist jeans stores for rustic shades of denim.

MOST FASHION CONSCIOUS PERSON —
Dame Edna Everage
George Michael
Prince
Jonathan Ross

W I N N E R

Prince — for flying in the face of convention and always setting the pace.
PRINCE — he thinks the sun shines out of his wardrobe!

THE PROCLAIMERS — Snap!

MOST IDENTICAL TWINS —
The Goss Twins
The Proclaimers
The Thompson Twins
The Cocteau Twins

W I N N E R

The Proclaimers — we still can't tell them apart!

BEN ELTON — More mouth than a dentist's waiting room!

U2 — nothing to sniff at!

KING — shortly afterwards, someone stole the microphone stand and he fell flat on his face!

MORRISSEY — no meat — all bones!

SINEAD O'CONNOR — a close shave for Des and Tom as they're brushed aside by Sinead!

MOST SUCCESSFUL BAND OF THE EIGHTIES —
U2
Bananarama
Def Leppard
Pet Shop Boys

W I N N E R

U2 — for making Island Records extremely rich!

BIGGEST FLOP OF THE EIGHTIES —
King
Sigue Sigue Sputnik
Nick Kamen
The Beastie Boys

W I N N E R

Sigue Sigue Sputnik. So bad, even Stock, Aitken and Waterman couldn't give them a hit!

MOST HERBIVOROUS PERSON —
Morrissey
Meatloaf
Howard Jones
Chris Lowe

W I N N E R

Morrissey — for outstanding service to vegetables.

BEST PERSON WITH THE SURNAME O'CONNOR —
Des O'Connor
Tom O'Connor
Sinead O'Connor
Sean O'Connery (?)

W I N N E R

Sinead O'Connor — for managing, against astounding odds, to still have less hair than anyone else.

THE JACKIE AWARDS FOR THE 80's

It was a fun occasion. The Jackie Awards Ceremony for Outstanding Prowess in all Fields of Entertainment! The judges scrutinised each of the nominees for each category very carefully and they took no prisoners (only cheques and Postal Orders!). Any appeals lodged will be treated with the respect they deserve — and filed diligently in the waste paper basket . . .

MOST WONDROUS SOAPS —
Neighbours
EastEnders
Brookside
Coronation Street

W I N N E R

Coronation Street — for producing no boring spin-off series or even more boring would-be pop stars.

FAVOURITE TELLY-STAR-TURNED-SINGER —
Nick Berry
Anita Dobson
Kylie Minogue
Bruce Willis

W I N N E R

Kylie Minogue — multi-talented, but very nice with it! A veritable goddess.

SMARMIEST PERSON ON TELLY —
Bob Monkhouse
Jonathan Ross
Jonathan King
Des O'Connor

W I N N E R

Joint winners : Bob Monkhouse/ Des O'Connor — for being able to persuade telly bosses to give them yet another series.

LEAST FASHION CONSCIOUS PERSON —
Paul King
Michael Jackson
Glenn Medeiros
Jonathan King

W I N N E R

Glenn Medeiros — need you ask why?

TELLY SNOOZE OF THE DECADE —
The Royal Weddings
Damon and Debbie
Wheel of Fortune
Wogan

W I N N E R

Wheel of Fortune — possibly the most boring game show ever.

FUNNIEST PERSON —
Ben Elton
Rowan Atkinson
Mel Smith
Victoria Wood

W I N N E R

Ben Elton — for Saturday Night Live, Friday Night Live, The Young Ones and Blackadder.

TOM JONES — Not just another hairy chest!

GEORGE MICHAEL — never trust a Greek wearing lifts!

DONAHUE — Just like Kilroy — but without the cosmetics!

SEAN PENN — the photographer's best friend!

MOST SENSATIONAL COME-BACK —
Tom Jones
Gary Glitter
Donny Osmond
Sandie Shaw

W I N N E R

Tom Jones — for not taking himself too seriously!

MOST SUCCESSFUL ARTIST OF THE EIGHTIES —
Madonna
Bruce Springsteen
Michael Jackson
George Michael

W I N N E R

George Michael — from dole queue to multi-millionaire recording artist.

TELLY EVENT OF THE DECADE —
Live Aid
J.R. being shot
Mandela Concert
Nationwide All-Night Television

W I N N E R

Nationwide All-Night Television — for bringing us Phil Donahue and Night Network, two truly brilliant shows.

ANGRY YOUNG MAN OF THE DECADE —
Rob Lowe
Mickey Rourke
Charlie Sheen
Sean Penn

W I N N E R

Sean Penn — for causing the increase in insurance premiums for Hollywood photographers!

FROM VINYL

...AND BACK

It seems you can't become a pop star these days without having a go at being a film star as well. But there is, it seems, a surprisingly short list of those who have made the transition without terminally embarrassing themselves. We look at those chart stars who pass the screen test . . .

WE'VE all, at one time or another, held aspirations to be a movie star and, if appearing on the silver screen is not your cup of tea, then that's probably because you'd rather be a rock star. Some people, however, just can't get enough of the limelight and insist on spending a lot of time and energy on being both.

It's thanks to this unfortunate pastime amongst famous pop stars that movie audiences have had to grit their teeth and tolerate the less than brilliant acting of the likes of Roy Orbison, Roger Daltrey, Bob Dylan, Bob Geldof and Prince.

But not all pop stars have had a brief flirtation with the cinema only to return to their recording studios with their guitars between their legs. Some have made the transition from concert stage to screen with at least a modicum of success and without holding themselves up to too much public ridicule in the process.

Perhaps one of the first to move from a singing career to an acting one without doing severe damage to both was none other than lil' ol' Elvis Presley. "Love Me Tender" was the first Elvis film ever and, despite the fact that it opened to mixed reviews in 1956, it was obvious to cinema audiences everywhere that the King of Rock 'n' Roll had a natural gift for acting. Elvis made an astonishing number of films in the years that followed, perhaps the most acclaimed of which were "King Creole" and "Jailhouse Rock". In the end though, Elvis tired of the kinds of roles he was being offered and, having failed to attract the serious parts he craved, turned his back on Hollywood forever to concentrate on his music.

The eternally young Cliff Richard was another one to offer mass appeal as a singer-turned-actor. During the early years of his singing career Cliff had been hailed as the "British Elvis" and, as if to emphasise the point, he was plunged into a series of "swinging" teenage musicals, most notably "Summer Holiday" and "The Young Ones".

In the former, Cliff played a young man, who, working for London Transport, decides to fill a double-decker bus with friends and head for the sun. Unfortunately, like Westlers hotdogs, there is only so much an audience can take, and Cliff later went back to what he did best (we don't think!).

David Bowie has become somewhat accomplished in his film rôles, so much so, in fact, that *he* now appears in *films* almost as often as his *records* do in the *charts*. Memorable Bowie performances include "The Man Who Fell To Earth", "The Hungry", "Merry Christmas, Mr Lawrence" and "Labyrinth". In the latter he played the Goblin King alongside a whole cast of Jim Henson puppets (just

TO CELLULOID

AGAIN!

to make sure he wouldn't be upstaged!).

A lady who's enjoyed mixed fortunes at the box office is none other than Queen Madonna the First. Maddy actually made her film debut in a well-dodgy flick called "A Certain Sacrifice", that was so, um, rude, that, when she became a famous songstress years later, she tried to stop the distribution of the film. She redeemed herself, however, when she appeared in the marvellous "Desperately Seeking Susan", though this did urge Madonna's co-star Rosanna Arquette to comment, "Madonna should really have learned to act before jumping into the movie game!" Oooh, bitch!

The abysmal "Shanghai Surprise" came next, closely followed by the marginally better "Who's that Girl?". After that though, Madonna turned her attention to a stage production . . . David Mamet's "Speed The Plow".

Now for a fine group of lads who, believe it or not, used to be quite big celebrities and enjoyed the success of one or two hit singles back in the sixties. But in movies like "A Hard Day's Night" and "Help" these Liverpudlian musicians who called themselves The Beatles also made a name for themselves as screen stars. Admittedly, John, Paul, George and Ringo actually played *themselves* in the films, but their cheeky grins and dry wit won over many a ticket-paying punter and ensured that the career of The Beatles was not to be marred by any naff musicals.

If ever someone from the music industry is to prove their real worth in films though, there's no better way to do it than by winning an Oscar. And that's exactly what Cher did in 1988 with her performance in "Moonstruck". Originally one half of the sixties singing duo "Sonny and Cher", she has made numerous film appearances down through the years in flicks like "Silkwood", "Mask" and "The Witches of Eastwick".

Our very own Phil Collins rather surprisingly gave up his millionaire life-style to go on the run as train robber Buster Edwards in "Buster". Phil came out relatively unscathed from this successful caper in which he starred alongside Julie Walters. Not only that, but the ex-Genesis man even got a hit record out of his first big-screen venture. Well, you can't say fairer than that . . .

With a strangely psychopathic look in his eye, a really cool set of leathers and without a bass guitar in sight was how Sting appeared to us in the Sci-Fi epic "Dune". Funnily enough, "strangely psychopathic" is how Sting has appeared to us in "Quadrophenia", "The Bride" and "Brimstone and Treacle". Be that as it may, he is still recognised as one of the few musicians who can deliver when it comes to a convincing performance in front of the cameras . . . as is to be seen in his latest effort, "Stormy Monday".

Of course, when you have singers that want to be actors, then it stands to reason that you're going to have actors that want to be singers — and usually with about as much success. Take for example British actor, Rupert Everett's short-lived singing success. Can't remember? Well, it's no wonder, it really was *that* short.

The odds being against him did not stop film star Lee Marvin, however, from making it to the top of the charts in 1970, with the wonderful "Wand'rin' Star" a tune taken from the film, "Paint Your Wagon".

Who knows, maybe one day we'll see Rick Astley as the new James Bond or even a multi-million pound Bros movie. It doesn't bear thinking about!

IN AND OUT OF LOVE

If you spend your days endlessly pulling petals off daisies, chanting "he loves me, he loves me not", save yourself time by following our slightly more comprehensive guide . . .

IT MUST BE LOVE

WHAT is love, anyway?
"You can't see it with your eyes, hold it in your hands.
But like the wind it covers all the land.
Strong enough to rule the heart of any man, this thing called love.
It can lift you up, it can put you down.
Take your whole world and turn it all around.
Ever since time nothing's ever been found that's stronger than love."

So goes a song by someone called Johnny Cash which sums up the love condition perfectly! Love . . . sigh! It's what we wistful, dreamy damsels yearn for. But it isn't one of life's little luxuries, you know. It's something every girlie needs, unless you truly want to be a starchy old spinster, that is!

In our white socks and skipping-rope years, the affections of our parents is suffice, but come the teen years, it's the attentions of a male chum that's sought.

So, if you're still looking forward to slipping into the love-pot with Mr v. Hunky Pants, here's what it's all about.

You Know You're In Love When . . .

. . . You willingly tidy your bedroom, walk your dad's whippet and do the family washing, with a smile on your face and the strains of the theme tune from "Dallas" skidding out of your larynx. (If there's no man on the scene, visit your local G.P. — it could be a mystery disease!)

. . . Much to your dad's wallet's annoyance, spend hours on the phone speaking to loverboy when you only saw him five minutes ago.

. . . Get up at six o'clock every morning to wash your hair, dry it, bendy-rod it, put on full make-up and a spotless school uniform, because you'll see him first period, in maths.

. . . You're nice to your pesky little upstart of a brother.

. . . You brush your teeth every hour, causing serious gum damage, in case you see him and he fancies a speedy spoon!

. . . You wear extra strong deodorant with triple splashings of your mum's very snoot perfume so you smell tulip-sweet!

. . . You don't get nearly enough sleep due to him keeping you out, you being on the phone to him till the early hours or because you can't stop thinking about his eyes, the colour of . . . the sea?

. . . You spend all your pocket money on cutesy little teddy bears with tee-shirts which say "I Love You, Cuddle Me", to send to him.

Love Songs

"Slave To Love" — Bryan Ferry
"Love And Affection" — Joan Armatrading.
"Say A Little Prayer" — Aretha Franklin.
"Be My Baby" — Ronettes.
"See Me" — Luther Vandross.
"Love Me Tender" — Elvis Presley.

What Are The Symptoms, Doc?

The results of over-fanciful thoughts or actions are rapid heartbeat, in some cases palpitations, leading to more frequent or laboured breathing (deep sighing to us, dears!).

An increase in blood pressure causes the cheeks to redden and a temperature rise. You begin to sweat — not tres romantic, admittedly, but necessary to keep the body temperature regulated and prevent spontaneous combustion.

All this blood surging round your veins and the threat of overheating can make you feel a trifle giddy.

We, the Jackie Love Machines, are tempted to believe that all the above happenings involve a good few calories — so being in love makes you lose weight. Oh, well, any excuse — heh, heh, heh.

"It's Only Puppy Love!"

That sort of comment will make you feel quite blee-some, but it might be just that. If you're quite young and this is your first relationship, you might enjoy the fact you're going out with someone, but, secretly, you're a bit scared by the whole thing. You convince yourself and everyone else that this is the real thing and, indeed, it is a form of love.

Puppy love is harmless as long as you don't do anything that you don't feel ready for. So, enjoy it while it lasts and who knows, it might turn out to be a lot more than everyone — including yourself — expected.

Secret Love

If you fancy someone but they don't know or realise it, maybe you should do something about it. The next time you see him, smile! Any guy will at least smile back at you. Don't throw yourself at him, but if you get the chance, start a conversation. Say 'hi' and smile again. If

the boy in question has a brain he'll take the initiative and speak. If he ignores you this is an early warning that the boy's a waste of time — or shy!

Even if you only exchange pleasantries, at least you've opened the door, who knows what might happen next?

The Path Of True Love . . .

No, oft it doesn't run too smooth. If you both get on really well but there's an outside factor blighting your happiness, it can be difficult to know what to do.

Ex-Girlfriends — Blast! There's very often an ol' flame who doesn't quite fancy being extinguished! There's only one way of dealing with rotten skeletons from his closet and that's ignore them! Whether she's trying to split you up or just can't let him go, if you ignore her and not let her get to you, you're home and dry. Just remember, if he wanted to go back out with her he would have and he wouldn't be going out with you, would he?

Parental Disapproval — If either, or both, sets of parents make it obvious they're not keen on this relationship, at least hear them out. Until you're 16 years old, your parents are responsible for you and can therefore legally prevent you from doing anything they don't agree with. As in most arguments where it looks like you're on the losing side, the art of compromising is indeed priceless. Look at your parents' point of view and try to come to some arrangement. Why not invite him round to meet 'the family' so at least they can see for themselves what a 'nice' boy he is?

They may not go so far as not letting you out or chauffeuring you to and from school. However, you may notice your dad being slightly over-protective of you. Remember you've always been his 'little girl' and he's always been the only male in your life. It may be hard for him to accept that you're a young lady who's wanting the company of a boy. But be as open and as affectionate towards your dad as you can (don't go over the top or he may become suspicious). That way, he'll find it easier to talk to you and trust you.

Long Distance Love

Although it's murder, it really does help if you know you'll be together again soon, whether it's for the weekend, end of term or indefinitely. But one thing is important, if it's meant to be, it'll last. While he's away, don't sit and mope. Get out with your friends, join a club and establish your own interests. That way when you do see him, you'll have lots to tell him and it won't be too overpowering when he's actually there.

LOVESICK
(Or when you're extremely fed up with love)

LET'S face it, life's not quite the same without a lush boy to squeal over — but it doesn't mean life's immediately brilliant with one! It's wrong to think boyfriends are passports to happiness; they're not. Being miserable because there's no-one special to share your last sweetie with is a waste of time. It's up to you to make yourself happy when you're not dating so that, when you do start going steady, you'll be a well-rounded person with other interests and avoid spoiling a potentially wondrous relationship by smothering your other half with slushsomeness!

This is all supposing you *want* to be held in love's impassioned clutches. Could be you've wised up to realising there are advantages to not being involved. Maybe right now you get more out of fun times with friends and indulging personal interests and ambitions — whether you aim to be the next Kylie or can't get enough karate classes! Well, congratulations, in discovering one of the most important secrets of the cosmos — contrary to the popular belief most girlies hold, boys *don't* make the world go round!

You Know You're Not In Love When . . .

. . . You'd rather tidy your bedroom, walk your dad's whippet and do the family washing than get taken for a snoot meal with HIM.

. . . Much to your dad's surprised delight, the phone bill's incredibly low due to you never returning any of the poor lad's calls!

. . . You let your hair get the greasies, stop wearing make-up and develop a fondness for clothes your mother wouldn't wear — because you don't care what he thinks of you.

. . . Your pesky little brother drives you more bananas than usual.

. . . You constantly indulge in cheese 'n' pickle crisps, chilli burgers, garlic bread and bombay mix so your breath puts him off puckering up!

. . . You wear too much cheapo perfume to put him off your scent!

. . . You go to bed early and constantly get ten out of ten on tests — swotting's more satisfying than seeing him!

. . . You resent buying him a bag of salt 'n' vinegar, never mind a brillsome birthday present — and tiny teds whose shirts squeal 'I love you' get right up your nose!

Not Very Lovey-Dovey Songs

"When Will I Be Famous?" — Bros
"Wishing I Was Lucky" — The Wets
"1999" — Prince
"The Sun Always Shines On TV" — A-ha
"Monkey" — George Michael
"The Locomotion" — Kylie Minogue

What Are The Symptoms This Time, Doc?

If you're a typical hoplessly-*not*-in-love girlie, seeing the object of your not hot desires, will no doubt, induce boredom, irritability, yawning and a deep dread of sharing confined places with the male in question. Your blood will not be at bubbling point with passion nor will your pupils dilate dramatically. The chances of you developing goose-bumps in excitement is as likely as you inviting your mum along to a swish disco.

You will remain cool, calm and collected and wonder how on earth a little thing like love has been known to reduce the most sensible specimens of your friends into quivering, jibbering wrecks . . .

However, just as you can be in different types of love, there's various backgrounds to not being in love, too.

"There's Other Fish In The Sea!"

He's lost that loving feeling and you're left drifting through life like death warmed up. You think your shattered heart will never mend from the traumatic break-up he's so casually caused. Thoughts other than what to do to get him back are beyond your capacity but after you've poured out all the hurt to your best mate for the forty-twelfth time, there's nothing left to do but dust yourself off and get on with things. Convert that wilting sadness into anger — he's the fool for letting you go! Don't let such an idiot blight your life — stick on a smile, take each day as it comes and gradually get back into circulation. Then when the time's right, you'll be ready to go fishing for a boy who'll give you a lesson in *real* love!

Just Good Friends

You and this guy like each other's company but don't like how everyone assumes you're dating! He's a real brick, a good sport, a great mate — but soul-mate, no. He makes you smile but doesn't cause sparks to fly between you. A platonic relationship like this does have its advantages, however. It means you'll have a useful male point of view at hand, a handy party partner and a protective big brother figure rolled into one. Only thing is, such 'friendships' have the habit of turning into the grand romances people labelled it all along! Or they can grow into awkward, one-sided affairs. The moral here is — enjoy it before the scales of friendship tip!

The More The Merrier!

Some girlies are just never satisfied! They might already have a dream of a boyfriend — cutesy, chirpy and true — but it's not enough. There's got to be excitement in the form of other laddies to chase and two-time. Until they get found out, they probably will have pots of fun meeting reams of boys — but love goes out the window until they realise you can't experience the real thing on anything other than a one to one basis. If you don't feel ready for anything heavier than casual dates, at least make your intentions clear! That way you won't lead anyone on or feel pressured to go steady when you're not ready and your reputation won't hurtle down the dumper!

The Rocky Road Of Non-Romance

Technically, you could be seeing someone but the amount of falling-out sessions you have mean your relationship's hanging on by a thread and you spend just as much — if not more — time not speaking. So not only do you feel lonely when you're on your own but poles apart when you're together. Since getting to know him, maybe you resent how much time he spends with his mates or he doesn't like the way you dress or something always seems to go wrong. Trying to keep it going when it's going nowhere will only lead to further hurt. Break loose — no relationship at all is much better than a bad one.

Bad Boys

Like holding onto a fizzled-out romance, it's also pretty pointless trying to capture that hunky guy who lets his utter gorgeousness make him a rascal with all the girls! Of course you can't help it if he makes you gulp with love but you can avoid chasing blindly after him if he has a lousy reputation. Anyway, if he genuinely likes you he'll come after you. Otherwise, transfer your affections to someone who's got more to give and been around a lot less!

Looking For Love

You're ready and waiting to fall madly and badly in lu-urve but for some reason it's just not happening! Despite hip hairstyles galore, vamping up your school uniform and diligently brushing up on the foxiest goals of Charlie Nicholas, he remains singularly unimpressed, sigh. Matters get steadily worse when all your mates start going steady and blabbing off about it.

It's not easy, but don't look down about the lack of males in your life or try too hard to attract one — both are sure ways of making boys run — in the opposite direction! Instead, concentrate on whatever else takes your fancy (!) then, just when you least expect it, you will, we promise, meet someone special! And isn't it fun not knowing what and who's round the corner?

SPLASH!

It wasn't the greatest plan I'd ever heard, but I had to admit, Donna's plans usually worked. And as far as meeting boys was concerned, I was no expert . . .

I LEANED shivering against the swimming pool wall, wishing I could just go home. And wishing I'd never told Donna about the lifeguard.

You could hear her coming a mile away, which wasn't surprising. The teachers didn't call her "Mouth Almighty" for nothing.

"Give me that back! Give me that back!" she screeched as she came careering round the corner with her brother Jason and a gang of his mates. They'd nicked her swimming stuff and were chucking it about.

I stood up and walked over to meet them.

"Hi, Sarah," Jason yelled over the noise.

"Hi," I said, laughing as I watched Donna flying backwards and forwards, trying to get her stuff back. "She's on form today."

He nodded and smiled. "Is she ever anything else?"

People thought it was strange that Donna and I were such good friends — we were so different. We'd always got on, though, right since primary school. Maybe it's true what they say about opposites.

"Oh, just bog off, will you, Martin?" Donna yelled, as she finally caught one end of her towel and her swimming stuff went spilling out on to the gravel.

But the next minute, her laughs had changed to cries of pain as she held on to her wrist.

"Are you all right?" Martin asked, worriedly. "Have you hurt yourself?"

He bent to help Donna pick up her things and she smiled gratefully, lowering her eyes at the same time.

Jason looked at me and we both turned away, smiling. We knew her too well to be worried about her 'injury'!

By the time all the lads had left through the turnstile, Donna was beaming like an idiot. And her wrist seemed to have mysteriously got better.

"Well, what d'you reckon, then?" she asked me, rolling her bikini up in the towel again.

"What about?"

"Martin, that new mate of Jason's. Not bad, eh? Reckon I could be in luck there, if I play my cards right."

"You mean he hasn't asked you out yet?" I said, in pretend surprise. "And you walked all the way here with him? You're slipping a bit, aren't you?"

She laughed. That's one good thing about Donna, anyway. She can always take a joke.

"Give us a chance," she said. "I've only known him ten minutes. Now if I'd had a quarter of an hour . . ."

She finished getting her stuff together and tucked it under her arm, laughing. "Right, then," she said finally. "All ready for Plan A?"

My heart sank. So she hadn't forgotten.

"Er, Donna . . . this lifeguard thing . . ." I began, and she looked at me.

"Yeah?"

"Well, I've been thinking. I'm not sure it's such a good idea."

"Oh, don't tell me your bottle's gone," she snapped, irritated.

"No, but you didn't tell Jason and that lot, did you?"

"Do me a favour, Sarah," she sighed. "What kind of friend do you think I am?"

There was no answer to that. I looked over to the swimming pool and gulped nervously.

"Look," Donna said, "do you want to get talking to this hunk of yours or not?"

"Yeah, but . . ."

"And have you got a better idea?"

I swallowed hard.

"No," I said. "I suppose not."

"Well?"

I thought for a moment. It was true. He was a bit on the delicious side, my lifeguard. And I was getting fed up of sinking into the woodwork all the time. I quite fancied being more like Donna, always assertive and extrovert.

"Oh, all right," I said eventually. "Go on then."

We went in separately, as if we didn't know each other. Past the café, past the lifeguard's chair, and up to the wooden changing rooms. Donna went in to one next to mine.

"Hey, I see what you mean," she whispered over the partition. "He's a bit tasty."

"Mmm," I said, trying to do up the back of my bikini top with shaking hands.

Actually, it was only luck that it wasn't Donna who'd seen him first. We'd been together at the pool the day before, until she got chatted up by this lad called Matthew.

"You don't mind, do you, Sarah?" she'd said, gathering up her things to go for a coffee with him.

"Do I ever?" I'd laughed, and she'd smiled at me.

"Ta. See you tomorrow then. I'll give you all the details."

It was true. I really didn't mind. Sometimes I even did quite well out of Donna's men! Not that day, though. Matthew's mate was four foot six and looked like Benny Hill!

I wasn't going to stay long after Donna left. But then I saw the lifeguard. And I changed my mind.

He walked out of the door marked "Staff" looking like he owned the place, muscles everywhere, and all those gorgeous teeth. I watched him climb in to his chair and stretch

out lazily in his little white shorts.

"Oh," I thought. "This is love."

I had to tell somebody. Had to. And Donna is supposed to be my best mate, even if she is completely cracked. How was I supposed to know what she was going to come up with?

"So what d'you reckon, then?" she'd said, excited, when she first thought of it. "Am I a super-brain, or what?"

"What?" I said.

"Oh, ha, ha," she said sarcastically. "No, come on, admit it, Sarah. It's brilliant."

I looked at Donna in amazement. Sometimes, I thought she hadn't changed since infant school!

"You are joking, I hope."

"No. Why? You want to get talking to him, don't you?"

"Yeah, but don't you think it's a bit sort of . . . obvious?"

Donna looked at me with that "know-it-all" expression she used so much.

"Ah," she said. "Well that depends on how you

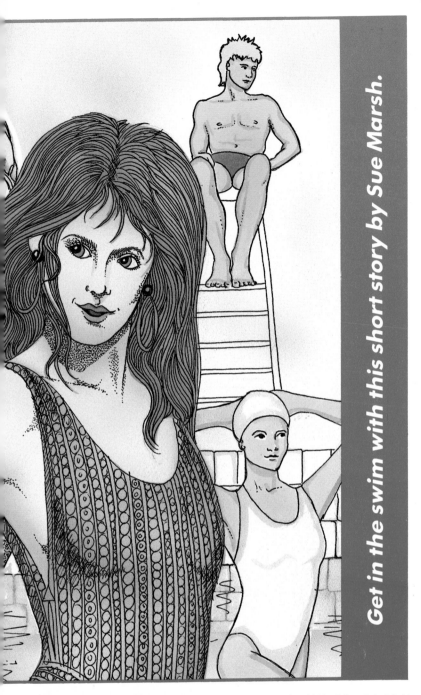

the deep end, next to this fat man doing handstands.

I sat on the side, slid in, and got to him just as he came spurting up from the bottom, spraying water out of his mouth. Very impressive, I thought sarcastically.

Looking round, I saw Donna watching me inconspicuously from the side. She gave a thumbs-up sign and began to make her way round the pool.

"Watch it!" I said, nearly getting a toe up the nose, but the fat bloke didn't hear me.

I swam round in a circle for a minute or two, treading water, then spotted Donna again. She'd nearly reached the big white chair where he sat, leaning back, his blond hair and brown skin shining in the reflected light of the pool.

Right, I thought, gulping nervously. Now or never. And I began to pad about in the water weakly, sinking a bit.

Out of the corner of my eye, I saw Donna by the white chair, looking over the pool. I lifted one of my arms up slightly, then let it down. At any time now, I thought, any time now. I sank down further, closing my eyes. And then I felt this arm come round me from behind.

"Aagh! No!" I gargled. "No . . ."

But the arm gripped me hard, trying to turn me round. He was too strong for me.

"No . . ." I glugged again, and a mouthful of chlorinated water went down my throat.

"It's OK," the fat man said, behind me. "I've got you." And I knew he had.

Well, that's that, I thought. I'll never get near my hunk now!

It seemed to take years to get back over to the side. I closed my eyes and tried not to imagine Donna cracking up with laughter as she saw me being towed in by the incredible bulk. I'd never live it down, that was for sure.

~~~~~

"OK? Are you OK?" he said when we got to the edge and he turned me round.

"Oh," I said. "Jason. I thought . . ."

"What?"

He was watching me through long dark lashes, his eyes deep brown and beautiful. And worried about me.

"Oh, nothing," I said, looking over his shoulder to where the big fat man was still doing acrobatics in the middle of the pool.

"Come on," he said. "I'll help you up the steps."

"Do you feel all right?" he said after a while, and I nodded. Neither of us spoke for a minute or two.

But then, "You know, it's funny . . ." we both said together, and stopped, smiling into each other's eyes.

Somehow, we didn't seem to need to say anything else. We just knew. When Jason put his arm round my waist I didn't move away. My head reached to his shoulder, and I laid it there. It felt nice.

I looked over to the high white chair on the other side of the pool, where Donna was laughing with the lifeguard, climbing up on the chair, giving him a bite of her Cornetto. She waved across to me, and I waved back.

"You know," Jason said, "they shouldn't let the lifeguards mess around like that. It's dangerous."

I didn't answer, just closed my eyes, enjoying the feeling of my cheek against his skin. I wondered why I'd never noticed him before. All these years, I thought. And he's always been just Donna's brother. Funny how things can turn out.

"And Donna's just as bad," he said. "Look at her. You could have drowned for all she cared."

"It doesn't matter," I said, looking up and smiling at him. "It doesn't matter, Jason."

And it really didn't.

THE END

do it. If all you do is throw yourself in at the deep end yelling 'Help! Help!', well, yeah, that would be a bit on the unsubtle side. But what if you just sort of started . . . drowning quietly."

"Drowning quietly?" It was beginning to sound like a typical Donna idea. "Er . . . look, Donna," I said, "I don't like to point this out, but first of all, drowning quietly doesn't sound like my ideal way of spending a Saturday afternoon, and secondly, the object was to get him to notice me, in case you'd forgotten. Not for me to spend the day wallying around with a mouth full of chlorine."

Donna shook her head.

"You just don't get it, do you?" she said. "You've forgotten about the casual person passing by the lifeguard's chair who just happens to notice you."

"Oh, I see." I said. "And this casual person — it wouldn't happen to be you, would it?"

She looked at me and smiled.

"You know, Sarah," she said, "you're not as thick as you look."

I don't know how I let her talk me in to it, but I did. And, shivering in the changing room, I really wished I hadn't.

"Right." I heard her voice over the partition again. "See you down there." And I heard the cubicle door close and her footsteps fading away.

~~~~~

By the time I'd given my hanger in and got the big rubber band with my number on, I was starting to wish I hadn't had any dinner. I walked over to the pool feeling decidedly queasy.

I saw Donna coming out of the café with a Cornetto. A boy smiled at her as she went past, but she didn't seem to notice. She's a good mate, I thought. She's only thinking about me. And that's when I decided to go through with it.

Taking a deep breath, I looked around the pool. There was only one place I could see where I'd be in easy view, and that was in the middle of

85

COLOUR STORY

YOU MAY LOVE FUCHSIA PINK EYESHADOW AND AZURE BLUE MASCARA, BUT IF YOU'RE A BLAZING REDHEAD THEY'RE NOT EXACTLY GOING TO FLATTER YOU! TAKE A TIP FROM US ON SHADES TO SUIT YOUR COLOURING.

BLONDES

Blondes nearly always have very fair skin, so heavy or dark make-up should be avoided. The same goes for deep tans — you'll look like a photographic negative! A light golden tan looks best with blonde hair.

Don't make the mistake of using a darker foundation than you really need, just to give you colour — your lipstick and eyeshadow will do that. So choose the shade of foundation nearest your own skin and dust it with some loose translucent powder.

Most blondes look great in pink so use a medium shade of pink over the whole of your eyelid. Then, blend a dark brown into your sockets and close to your upper lashes. Using a fine brush, lightly stroke just under the lower lashes with the brown. Dark brown mascara will open the eyes and won't look as harsh and false as black.

Lipstick should be pale and pastel or strong, but definitely not dark.

BRUNETTES

Dark-haired girls can afford to wear deeper and more vibrant tones than blondes, although very dark colours should be kept for evenings. After applying your foundation, finish off with a light dusting of translucent powder, or a tinted powder if your skin is fairly dark.

Shades of mauve, lilac and deep purple all look good on you but for the daytime, a medium pink shade of eyeshadow and a deep lilac are strong enough.

A touch of rosy blusher high on your cheekbones will warm up your cheeks and draw attention to your eyes, while a strawberry pink lipstick will add the finishing touch.

REDHEADS

Most redheads have pale skin and freckles which they're always trying to cover up. Well, don't! Nothing looks worse on a fair skin than thick layers of heavy foundation. Freckles can be very attractive, so make the most of them.

Use a light liquid foundation and a translucent powder, then warm up your face with a tawny blusher.

Shades of rust (so long as they're not too orangey) look great on redheads. We used a fairly light rust all over the eyelid and a darker brown shadow to create soft smudgy lines close to both the upper and lower lashes.

A pale peachy lipstick with just a touch of tinted gloss finishes this natural look.

DRESSED TO KILL
(you'll die laughing)!

It's happened to all of us at one time or another, hasn't it, girlies? You invite your new boyfriend to meet your parents or boogie on down at the local disco for the first time so you can show him off to all your mates — and he turns up in the most hideous clothes you've ever seen.

Even worse, when you scream, "What on earth are you wearing?" he only stares at you uncomprehendingly. These are his best clothes, for heaven's sake!

So, if you think there's even the slightest chance of your lad ever giving you a showing-up on an important occasion, take our advice and warn him now that it's the last thing he'll ever do! Better still, take the first opportunity to go through his wardrobe, find whatever horrific creations might be lurking in its murky depths and toss 'em binwards. It could save you a lot of embarrassment!

And if you're not sure exactly what you're looking for, just read the following Jackie guide to total naffness. It should leave you in no doubt as to whether your guy is dripping with street cred — or just a drip . . . !

Chances are, the first time you meet your new boyfriend-to-be, he'll be dressed fairly normally. I mean, you're not exactly going to be bowled over by someone in cord flares, are you? Or maybe you're just so gob-smacked by his big brown eyes and intoxicating personality that you don't actually notice the gold medallion nestling in his chest wig!

Even on your first few dates, it's likely he'll take extra-special care with his appearance, but by the time you've known each other a week, the effort will probably have got too much for him.

That's when he may:
turn up at your house for tea in ripped denims, Doc Marten boots and an Iron Maiden t-shirt with sweat marks under the arms. Considering the last time you saw him, he'd come straight from his job at the bank and was wearing a pin-stripe suit, this comes as a bit of a shock to you — and even more of a shock to your mum!

Other accessories he'll be sporting may include leather-studded wristbands, a couple of toilet chains and a leather jacket emblazoned with the (untruthful) boast "I eat children for breakfast" or some other similarly endearing claim to fame. It's going to take all your powers of persuasion to convince your mother he's really a big softie underneath!

Or, he might:
turn up at the disco in skin-tight leather trousers, shirt unbuttoned to the navel, dripping with more gold than the Queen Mum and sporting a mysterious growth on his chin which is meant to be designer stubble but looks more like a five o'clock shadow.

He won't make any comment on the slinky, black number you've bought specially for the occasion, mainly because he hasn't noticed what you're wearing. But you'd better ditch those high heels straight away, as he'll have you strutting your funky stuff on the dance floor all night — so that there's no danger of anyone missing him in his groovy gear.

This boy could be a normal human being by day, but show him a darkened room, flashing lights and a crowded dance floor (or an empty one — it's all the same to him!) and suddenly it's Joey Boswell meets Wayne Sleep! Just make sure you get him home by twelve o'clock or he could turn into a pumpkin — some of your friends might think he's one already!

Alternatively, he could:
arrive at your cousin's wedding in a brown suit with six-inch wide lapels and flared turn-ups that don't quite reach his ankles. "Matching" accessories are a purple kipper tie, black nylon socks and white slip-on shoes. As you gaze at him in stunned silence, he assumes you're lost in admiration and puffs his chest out with pride, causing a button to ping off his jacket!

Don't be too hard on him — he probably hasn't worn a suit since the last wedding he was at when he was a page boy and the black velvet number he wore then doesn't fit him now. Trouble is, neither does the one he's wearing because it's not actually his — he had to borrow it from his dad who's two sizes smaller than him!

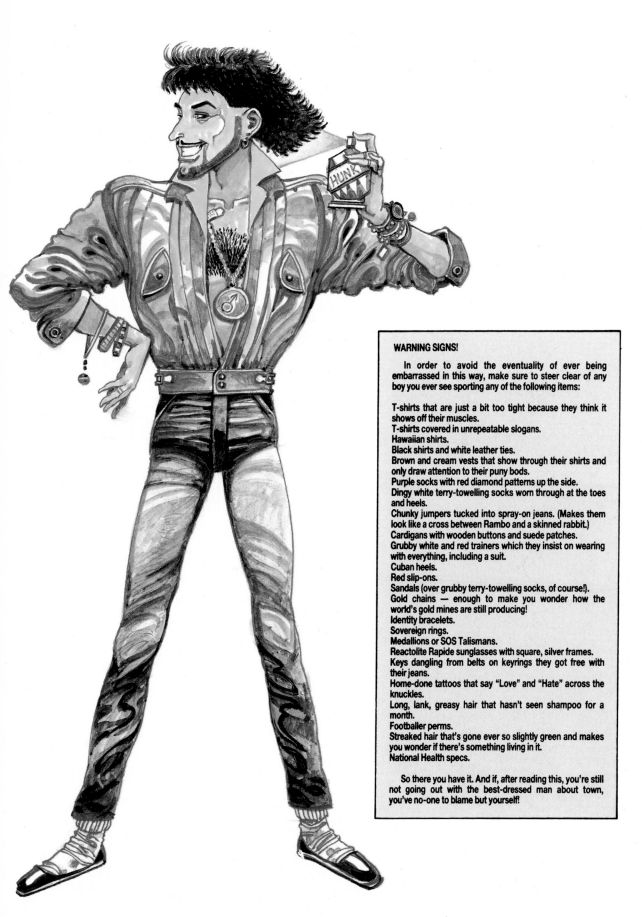

WARNING SIGNS!

In order to avoid the eventuality of ever being embarrassed in this way, make sure to steer clear of any boy you ever see sporting any of the following items:

T-shirts that are just a bit too tight because they think it shows off their muscles.
T-shirts covered in unrepeatable slogans.
Hawaiian shirts.
Black shirts and white leather ties.
Brown and cream vests that show through their shirts and only draw attention to their puny bods.
Purple socks with red diamond patterns up the side.
Dingy white terry-towelling socks worn through at the toes and heels.
Chunky jumpers tucked into spray-on jeans. (Makes them look like a cross between Rambo and a skinned rabbit.)
Cardigans with wooden buttons and suede patches.
Grubby white and red trainers which they insist on wearing with everything, including a suit.
Cuban heels.
Red slip-ons.
Sandals (over grubby terry-towelling socks, of course!).
Gold chains — enough to make you wonder how the world's gold mines are still producing!
Identity bracelets.
Sovereign rings.
Medallions or SOS Talismans.
Reactolite Rapide sunglasses with square, silver frames.
Keys dangling from belts on keyrings they got free with their jeans.
Home-done tattoos that say "Love" and "Hate" across the knuckles.
Long, lank, greasy hair that hasn't seen shampoo for a month.
Footballer perms.
Streaked hair that's gone ever so slightly green and makes you wonder if there's something living in it.
National Health specs.

So there you have it. And if, after reading this, you're still not going out with the best-dressed man about town, you've no-one to blame but yourself!

BEAT THE BULGE!

There's nothing worse than that terrible sinking feeling you get when you step on to the scales for the first time in several weeks — and watch, horrified, as the needle shoots way beyond the point where you expected it to stop! Or when you try to slip in to your favourite jeans only to discover that no matter how much you roll about on the carpet, there's no way you're going to get the zip up!

Perhaps your first reaction is to rush to the biscuit tin in a fit of pique, demolish half a packet of Gypsy Creams, then spend the rest of the evening in front of the telly instead of at the disco as you'd originally intended. (Who'd want to dance with a fat slob like you, anyway?) Well, we can sympathise, but feeling sorry for yourself is only going to make things worse.

Of course, the best advice we can give you is to always eat a balanced diet and take regular exercise so the problem of being overweight never arises. However, the lure of chocolate, crisps and cream cakes is too strong for most of us! So if you're now in the unhappy position of wanting to lose a few pounds but haven't a clue how to go about it, here are a few tips that will hopefully point you in the right direction!

1. If you're very overweight and want to lose several pounds very quickly, aim to eat no more than 1000 calories a day. For more gradual weight loss (and remember, the slower you lose it, the more likely it is to stay off) aim to restrict your intake to between 1200 and 1500 calories a day.

2. Cut out all fatty and sugary snacks such as crisps, chips and sweets. You could lose weight on a diet of three Mars Bars a day, but your skin, hair and general appearance would suffer dreadfully and you'd find you had very little energy. Make sure your daily quota of calories is taken from a wide range of wholesome foods so that your body still gets the daily nutrients it needs to function properly.

3. Try to eat more than half your daily allowance in the first half of the day. Your evening meal should be a light snack — and never eat after 8 o'clock at night.

4. Cut down on salt as it makes your body retain water. Use herbs and spices instead.

5. Arrange your slimline meals on smaller plates to make them look bigger! Drink a glass of water before you start to eat as this will curb the hunger pangs and make you want less. Chew your food slowly, savour each mouthful and don't be distracted by the TV, or you'll suddenly look down on an empty plate and wonder where the food's gone!

6. Write down everything you have to eat each day — even if it's only a chip you pinched off your friend's plate! This will make you less likely to cheat. Don't be misled by the popular belief that a chocolate bar doesn't count if no-one sees you eating it!

7. Don't be put off if you don't lose half a stone overnight. The longer you persevere, the easier it will get as your appetite will shrink, you'll stop craving sugar and the loss of even a few pounds will be a real incentive to lose more.

8. Don't think that dieting means miserable weeks living on cardboard crispbreads and damp lettuce leaves. Take time to prepare appetising, healthy meals using plenty of fresh fruit, vegetables and herbs. You'll discover a lot of tempting nosh which you might actually prefer to the daily stodge you were used to.

9. Find a photograph of yourself when you were at your ideal weight and stick it on the fridge door or biscuit-tin lid to remind you of what the struggle's all about. Alternatively, use a picture of a very fat person to scare yourself into submission!

10. It's very important to take some form of daily exercise when you're dieting, not only because it uses up extra calories and speeds up your body's metabolism, but also because it tightens up skin which would otherwise become loose and flabby with sudden weight loss.

And remember, when you reach your ideal weight, don't decide to lose another half stone. Concentrate on maintaining your new weight. Remember it is dangerous to over-diet, and no one's going to be impressed if you end up resembling a stick insect!

HOLLYWOOD

RITA • HAYWORTH

CLASSICS

P·A·A·A

Feel like throwing a party? It could be a lot of fun, but on the other hand, if you don't do your homework, it could be a total disaster!

But, never fear. Just follow the Jackie guide to party success and you'll soon earn a reputation as the hostess with the mostest . . .!

WHEN TO PARTY?

What do you mean, when to party? Hey, any time is party time and practically anything is something to celebrate if it'll give you an excuse to push back the furniture, get a few friends round and have a boogie!

Remember, though — even if you think the ideal time to party is RIGHT NOW, everyone else might not share your enthusiasm! For instance, your parents, brothers, sisters, dog, cat and budgie might not take too kindly to having their evening in front of the box disturbed by you, your pals and a pile of Pet Shop Boys albums. So, the ideal solution is to get rid of your family for the evening.

If they're not too keen to leave you and your chums alone in the house, ask them if they'd mind spending the evening in another room in the house, leaving you all to enjoy yourselves but being close enough to sort out any problems.

WHO TO INVITE

Once you've got the go-ahead, it's important to decide just how many guests you're planning on. Perhaps your mother doesn't quite relish the thought of four hundred people stamping around her 12' x 12' sitting room, but, on the other hand, if you live in a bit of a snoot mansion, six guests might feel just a little bit lost!

Anyway, once you've decided on numbers, you'll have to let people know about your party.

The obvious way to do this, of course, is to hand out invites. They don't necessarily have to be cards — just quick notes telling people the place, date and time is enough. Or you could always just spread the news! Tell your friends, and ask them to tell their friends — the word usually gets round.

It's best to tell everyone as far in advance as possible. That way, there's a better chance that they won't have anything else

-RTY!

planned and you won't end up sitting alone in a room full of salted peanuts and enough glasses to build a full-scale model of Crystal Palace!

Also, make sure you invite a good mix of guests. The party might not be an outrageous success if four out of five guests are girls and, equally, things might be a little obvious if there's just you, your two best mates and twenty boys!

A couple of days before the party, it's a good idea to ask around to see who's going to make it and who isn't — that way you'll know roughly how many people to expect and how much food you're going to need!

It's best to keep the food fairly simple — sandwiches, crisps and peanuts will be fine. Or, if you're a bit more adventurous, try some bread sticks and sliced raw vegetables with dips.

PARTY TIME

The great day has come! The parents have disappeared, the neighbours have barricaded their front doors, the furniture has been pushed back, there's a table of tempting tasties on offer and your dad has removed his Jim Reeves albums to a place of safety. The friends that came round to help you get ready are putting on a few party dance records.

So, what next?

* Don't worry if you don't find fifty people camped on your doorstep at eight o'clock — a lot of people think it's very uncool to turn up at a party on time!
* When people do start to arrive, try to speak to everyone that you've invited, even if it's only for a short while. It's only polite, and they'll feel more comfortable knowing they're welcome and so are more likely to enjoy themselves.
* If there's a lot of people who don't know each other, waste no time introducing them. There's nothing worse for a party than a room full of people who don't know each other.
* Don't get uptight when you see people rolling all over the sofa, crisps being ground into the carpet and a general mess being made. You can always tidy up later and people aren't likely to enjoy a party when the hostess is constantly screaming, "Don't make a mess!"
* It's usually a good idea to have one person, or even a few people taking turns to deal with the music. That way, your records (and the ones taken by other people) won't get scratched to pieces.
* Should someone decide to turn up even though you hadn't invited them, don't make a scene! If you know them and they're OK, the chances are they just want to join in the fun and, besides, the more the merrier! But if it's someone you don't know or someone you don't want around, ask them politely to leave and if that doesn't work, threaten to phone the police.

THE AFTERMATH

It's a good idea to have a few people who are willing to help tidy up after everyone else has left. A house can look pretty devastated after a good party, but fear not, for it usually looks a lot worse than it really is and the more people you get to help tidy up, the sooner things will get back to normal.

Then comes the best bit! The day or two that follows a party are usually the best for gossip, scandal and the kind of juicy morsels that you and your friends can talk about for hours! Happy partying!

TEN GOOD TIMES TO HAVE A PARTY
1. When it's your birthday!
2. When it's your tortoise's birthday!
3. When it's Christmas/New Year/Hallowe'en/Guy Fawkes!
4. When you want to get your paws on that guy in 5C!
5. When the cat's had kittens!
6. When you've passed your exams!
7. When you've failed your exams!
8. When George Michael's back at number one!
9. When it's any day with a "y" in it!
10. When there's nothing on the TV!

TEN GREAT PARTY RECORDS
1. Twist And Shout — The Beatles
2. Tutti Frutti — Little Richard
3. Into The Groove — Madonna
4. C'mon Everybody — Eddie Cochran
5. Louie Louie — The Fat Boys
6. Shout — Lulu
7. It's My Party And I'll Cry If I Want to — Dave Stewart and Barbara Gaskin
8. Blue Suede Shoes — Elvis Presley
9. Prime Mover — Zodiac Mindwarp
10. Can Can — Bad Manners

TEN PEOPLE YOU WOULDN'T INVITE TO A PARTY
1. Cliff Richard
2. Robocop
3. Sean Penn
4. Terry Wogan
5. Simon Bates
6. Emma Ridley
7. Steve Davis
8. Frank Bruno
9. Rick Astley
10. A Proclaimer

TEN GREAT PARTY GUESTS
1. Eddie Murphy
2. Jason Donovan
3. Dawn French
4. Matthew Broderick
5. Bros
6. The school football team
7. Lenny Henry
8. Bruce Willis
9. George Michael
10. Anyone that looks worse than you in a mini skirt

Those
G★O★L★D★E★N

THE BEST . . . AND THE WORST

There were lots of good things around in the 80's, but an awful lot of not-so-good things too. Here's just a few . . .

FAVOURITE ACTORS
Rob Lowe
Bruce Willis
Emilio Estevez
Michael Douglas
Kiefer Sutherland

FAVOURITE ACTRESSES
Melanie Griffith
Demi Moore
Molly Ringwald
Joanne Whalley-Kilmer
Kelly McGillis

BEST FASHIONS
Doc Martens
Stonewashed Jeans
Boxer Shorts
Zoot Suits
Waistcoats

WORST FASHIONS
Leg Warmers
Puffball Skirts
Smiley T-shirts
Anything in Lamé
Frocks for Men

BEST TV PROGRAMMES
Network Seven
Spitting Image
Night Network
Saturday/Friday Night Live
Moonlighting

WORST TV PROGRAMMES
Blind Date
Surprise Surprise
Trick Or Treat
Bob's Full House
Mr & Mrs

BEST SOAP
Crossroads
Take The High Road
Neighbours
Brookside
EastEnders

WORST SOAP
Dancing Days
Emmerdale Farm
Young Doctors
A Country Practice
Prisoner: Cell Block H

FAVOURITE TV PERSONALITIES
Keith Floyd
Julian Clary
Phillip Schofield
Jonathon Ross
Muriel Gray

LEAST FAVOURITE TV PERSONALITIES
Bernard Manning
Des O'Connor
Terry Wogan
Robert Kilroy-Silk
Judith Chalmers

FAVOURITE BANDS
Wet Wet Wet
Duran Duran
Bros
Bon Jovi
Bananarama

LEAST FAVOURITE BANDS
Dollar
Bucks Fizz
Zodiac Mindwarp
Goombay Dance Band
The Pogues